"Here, in a brief and highly readable form, is a fascinating and amazingly comprehensive catalog of the many puzzling and significant global forces in our present world. Here are no simplistic proposals, rather foundational grist for the mill of the fearless believer. These facts won't wear out."

—Ralph D. Winter, Ph.D.,
General Director, U. S. Center for World Mission

HURTLING TOWARD OBLIVION

HURTLING
TOWARD
OBLIVION

**A LOGICAL
ARGUMENT
FOR THE END
OF THE AGE**

RICHARD A. SWENSON, M.D.

NAVPRESS

BRINGING TRUTH TO LIFE

P.O. Box 35001, Colorado Springs, Colorado 80935

The Navigators is an international Christian organization. Our mission is to reach, disciple, and equip people to know Christ and to make Him known through successive generations. We envision multitudes of diverse people in the United States and every other nation who have a passionate love for Christ, live a lifestyle of sharing Christ's love, and multiply spiritual laborers among those without Christ.

NavPress is the publishing ministry of The Navigators. NavPress publications help believers learn biblical truth and apply what they learn to their lives and ministries. Our mission is to stimulate spiritual formation among our readers.

ISBN 1-57683-070-5

Swenson, Richard A.
    Hurtling toward oblivion : a logical argument for the end of the age / by Richard A. Swenson.
        p.   cm.
    ISBN 1-57683-070-5   (pbk.)
    1. End of the world.   I. Title.
BT876.S94   1999
236'.9 — dc21   98-55913
                                                  CIP

Printed in the United States of America

2 3 4 5 6 7 8 9 10 11 12 13 14 15 / 05 04 03 02 01

FOR A FREE CATALOG OF
NAVPRESS BOOKS & BIBLE STUDIES,
CALL 1-800-366-7788 (USA)
OR 1-416-499-4615 (CANADA)

To our sons

Adam and Matt

Your generation will surely witness interesting days.
My advice: don't quit . . . just live ready. Conduct your studies
with diligence, your work with perseverance, and your
realtionships with grace. Seek authenticity at the highest level,
for one of the great gifts of authenticity is that it leaves us
continuously ready for "what comes next."

CONTENTS

PREFACE

One day as I was driving down I-94 near my home in Wisconsin, my thoughts shocked me into pulling over to the side of the road. All of a sudden, without warning and without specific intention, my mind had sequenced several future trends in such a way that the end of the age seemed unavoidable. Before the idea could disappear into a *poof* of cerebral vapor, I quickly slammed the car into park, tore off a scrap of paper, and frantically began writing. There I sat— probably illegally—along a stretch of rural Wisconsin interstate, traffic flying by at 70 miles per hour. But I had forgotten everything else, instead fully concentrating on recording my thoughts while at the same time shaking my head in astonishment and disbelief. *Is history really rounding the last lap for the homestretch?* I wondered.

I have no idea why my brain processed in the way it did. I had not previously taken more than a passing interest in doomsday scenarios. Among the thousands of books in my library, I doubt if I owned a single volume on the topic. I had no emotional investment that desired the destruction of the world. I had no preconceived theological position that was benefited by such end-times reasoning (except, perhaps, that I believed history to be linear, not cyclical). As a matter of fact, although I am a spiritually minded person, eschatology was the last part of my theology to fall into place. Without much effort, I basically agreed with C. S. Lewis's statement: "As a Christian I take it for granted that human history will some day end; and I am offering Omniscience no advice as to the best date for that consummation."[1] Rather, what happened on the side of the road was seemingly unprovoked: simple, straightforward, and objective. And the conclusion was stark and unavoidable—the world is on a treadmill to oblivion.

Let me back up a few years and explain how all this got started. I am a physician, but I am also a cultural analyst and a futurist (with an undergraduate degree in physics, which will assume more relevance later). Discerning the times is my passion. Understanding the big picture is what I do best. Such activities have long been my avocation, and I have spent tens of thousands of hours over the past decades attempting to understand *what* is happening in the world, *why* it is happening, and *where* it is leading us. In preparation for various presentations and writing projects, I had researched, analyzed, synthesized, and categorized fifty trends that were propelling American society—and increasingly, the entire world—along its path to the future.

As I was cruising down this beautiful stretch of highway, however, I was not particularly thinking about future trends. I was not intellectually occupied with cracking any cosmic code, solving any international geopolitical problem, or fomenting any religious revolution. I was just . . . cruising. Perhaps looking at cloud formations. Perhaps scanning the edge of the woods for deer.

My brain, however, is often a poorly controlled explosion. On this sunny afternoon, unbeknownst to me, that same wandering, unruly, independent brain had its own agenda. Operating under its own instructions, it was busy postulating a putative final cliff for the world system to tumble over. It sequenced several of these previously identified future forces into a scenario that led to an inescapably disastrous consequence: The world is spinning out of control and approaching a threshold of lethality—a point where life as we know it can no longer continue. And if you are willing to accept my premises, I am willing to prove it to you. This book, then, is offered as a conceptualized proof that irreversible trends, principles, and forces currently at work in the world system (that is, the global environment where everything is connected to everything else) are inevitably propelling us toward a cataclysmic outcome.

This side-of-the-road experience lightning bolted my life in 1994. Since that day I have given oblivion plenty of time to change its mind and swallow the proof rather than the world system. But the proof has shown itself remarkably resilient. If anything, it has gotten stronger, fed insatiably by each new raw bit of evidence flowing from the data-gathering systems of the world. I now routinely scan the news and say, "This is unbelievable!" Almost on a daily basis, new forceful signs emerge to strengthen my conviction that this empiric argument is both valid and binding.

Despite my strong convictions about its content, this book is advanced with several significant hesitations:

Redundancy—You might be asking yourself: *Does the world really need another end-times book?* There are hundreds of books on this topic already, both religious and secular—some frantically warning, others frantically debunking. This book, however, claims to bring a new perspective to the debate and new evidence to the courtroom.

Counter-productivity—Some worry that all this doom-saying distracts us from working to make things better. Hope, they contend, is an important ingredient in efforts to improve the future. Taking away hope might perversely contribute to making the doom come true—the notorious self-fulfilling prophecy. Already in 1972, for example, British scientist John Maddox warned against scientific gloom authors (such as Paul Erhlich, Rachel Carson, and Barry

Commoner) by observing: "There is a danger that much of this gloomy foreboding about the immediate future will accomplish the opposite of what its authors intend. Instead of alerting people to important problems, it may seriously undermine the capacity of the human race to look out for its survival."[2] It is not my intention that people withdraw from life, from problem-solving, or from working for the common good. I wish to alert people—but certainly not to plunge them into a paralyzing counter-productive depression.

Skepticism—Perhaps many people are growing weary and cynical of all this end-times talk. Yelling "Wolf!" too often will do that. The apocalypse has been predicted for several millennia now, yet here we still sit on the veranda sipping our tea and yawning in derision. The sky hasn't fallen yet. *Why, it doesn't even appear to be sagging!* Instead, all those prophets of gloom are "going through the humiliation of being rung up by the newspapers and asked what they plan to have for lunch on the day after the day they predicted so firmly as the last in the history of the world."[3] I can't say I blame the holders of such skepticism. To an extent, I share in it. And I fear contributing to it.

Date setting—Many prophets have predicted The End will come on such an hour of such a day in exactly such a way. Personally, I think date setting is not only impossible, it is also credibility-shattering. I have no specific dates in mind. Instead of *an ominous date*, I am talking about *an ominous process* that will— as the process advances—cause the world system to inevitably spin out of control.

Emotionalism—When discussing apocalyptic scenarios, people can get worked into a frothy lather. Such excitability, however, often results in irrationality rather than enlightenment. It is important therefore that the thesis of this book be regarded with as much objectivity as possible. Please try to consider it without becoming too emotionally involved. Realizing how misleading feelings can be, try to check them at the door. Detachment of this kind is easier to talk about than achieve. I myself will surely wander over the objectivity line from time to time, probably scarcely noticing that it has happened. I apologize in advance.

Overreaction—We have all heard the stories: people selling everything and moving to a hilltop awaiting the stroke of midnight on The Day; people building bomb shelters with perimeter fences and equipping themselves with night vision goggles and Uzis; people committing mass suicide in a ritual pact. And at times there is a fraction of rational substance behind such hysteria in that end-times material is by its essence dramatic stuff. But such reactionary impulsivity is not an appropriate response to this book. As someone once said, "We should *live* as if each day were our last, but *plan* as if we were going to still be here one hundred years from now." My advice: go to college, start families, have children, build churches, and invest in community. Don't put the future on hold. Just get ready, stay ready, discern the times, live intentionally (not on autopilot), be humble, and always do what's right. Prioritize according to the transcendent rather than the temporal. That's not overreacting—it's merely living as we should have from the beginning.

Optimism/Pessimism—Optimists and pessimists often don't get along. Truthfully, I don't want to go anywhere near their perennial tug-of-war, as I undoubtedly will get tangled in their rope just as it snaps taut. But there is probably no way to avoid the debate.

This book actually has little to do with either optimism or pessimism. Ultimately, the only thing that matters is whether the thesis is true, and neither optimism nor pessimism will determine that outcome. There were undoubtedly optimists on the Titanic who drowned while gurgling, "This can never happen!" And there were undoubtedly pessimists on the Titanic who were rescued while gasping, "All is lost!" In the end, the fate of the world will not be determined by our view of things, but instead by the truth of things. We do not judge that truth—it always judges us.

Sensationalism—Hysteria brings fire to the eyes and acid to the stomach. Hype brings notoriety. Sensationalism brings a tabloid kind of success. Anyone who knows me understands just how personally alarming such a prospect is. (A hint—I score 19:2 on the introvert:extrovert scale.) Not wanting to jump on any such exploitative bandwagon, it is with a certain hesitancy that I go public with my thesis. Yet at this point, I feel to not do so would be irresponsible.

These are hesitations and concerns I have wrestled with for half a decade. But as each year passes, such wrestling becomes increasingly self-centered. What if, for example, I had known about the faulty O-rings yet did nothing to alert NASA about the impending Challenger explosion for fear of controversy? (This is, by the way, precisely what happened—there were several who feared this defect in the space shuttle design but were hesitant to push hard with their concerns.) What if I were the only person who understood in advance the potential devastation with Saving & Loan deregulation but didn't want to unduly alarm all those institutions and corporations? What if I knew Japan's planes were on their way to Pearl Harbor . . . or I saw Lee Harvey Oswald leave his house with a rifle, heading in the direction of a presidential motorcade? In each case, if I stood up and yelled, "Disaster!" it would have been controversial, sensationalistic, and, on a personal level, it would have disrupted my peaceful existence. But, on the other hand, to do nothing would have been not only irresponsible but unthinkable.

Let's take an illustration from the world of medicine. As a physician, I realize full well my patients' mortality. All people eventually get sick; all patients eventually die. Most clinic visits, however, are for completely benign complaints. Physicians spend far more time reassuring patients than alarming them. Most ailments resolve spontaneously. The body is largely self-correcting—as is the world system.

But this does not mean I can afford to fall asleep as a diagnostician, for sooner or later true disease erupts with a vengeance. When it does, I have to be ready. Just because last year's chest pain wasn't a heart attack doesn't mean today's chest pain isn't a serious threat to life. Just because last year's abdominal pain wasn't cancer doesn't mean today's abdominal pain isn't malignant. Once the pain is proven benign I will attempt to reassure—even if the patient isn't inclined to accept my reassurances. On the other hand, once the pain is proven serious I will attempt to sound the alarm—even if the patient is foolishly in denial. The more the denial, the more alarm bells I have to push to get the job done.

The issue for my patients is the *truth* of their symptoms. The issue for the world is the same. Just because yesterday's symptoms were misdiagnosed does not mean that today's symptoms should not be regarded seriously. Just because yesterday's findings were benign does not mean the world is invincible. Symptoms must be accounted for. Precise diagnostics are essential. Sooner or later, even neurotics get sick. Sooner or later, even hypochondriacs die.

Any attempted proof for the end of the age will unquestionably and understandably be controversial. This, I suppose, is unavoidable. While I *do* mean to provoke discussion, I have no interest in inciting hysteria or marketing sensationalism. *But if something is going down on our generational shift, it is our responsibility to confront it.* And if the evidence outlined here is valid, then it deserves to be circulated—no matter how controversial or discomforting.

If the sequential proof offered in the following pages is true, then such a thesis presents the entire human race with a sobering agenda. As Samuel Johnson pointed out centuries ago, "Depend on it. When a man knows he is going to be hanged in a fortnight, it concentrates his mind wonderfully." In the same way, the prospect of seriously facing the end times brings the flow of history into sharper perspective, straightening out temporal priorities with a sudden jerk.

If our global Titanic is nearing a cosmic iceberg, personally I want to know. If the world system is rushing toward collapse, truth matters. If the time for sipping tea on the veranda is over, then let's move on to the things that matter most.

CHAPTER ONE

AN INTRODUCTION TO THE FUTURE WE MIGHT NOT HAVE

"It is the business of the future to be dangerous," observed philosopher Alfred North Whitehead.[1] Seldom has business been so good. For a world system grown accustomed to living on the edge of a geopolitical nervous breakdown, the future is simultaneously celebrated and feared—both with good reason.

When we think of the future, what images do we see? Will it be a utopian dream or a nuclear nightmare? Will it be Shangri-La or Rwanda? "I have lived seventy-seven years . . . and I know I am old because the century was once rich in utopias that are now meaningless," wrote the late journalist and author Alfred Kazin. "What has not remained *anywhere* is the 'utopian' drive and confidence in the future that sparked the early 20th century."[2]

Before the nuclearization of the modern era, much of the literature of science fiction dealt with the promise of a glorious technological future. Today such optimism is seldom seen. Forty years ago, Hollywood's futuristic movies were utopian. Now they are all apocalyptic. "This is the first age that's paid much attention to the future," commented science fiction writer Arthur C. Clarke, "which is a little ironic since we might not have one."

The future "we might not have" is the topic under exploration in this book. There is substantial and credible evidence to suspect a cataclysm. It is not my intention to predict the *when*, *where*, or *who* of this cataclysm—but it is my explicit intention to explain the *why*. Thus, this is more a book about process than about details— a process that has clamped us in its jaws and is not about to let go.

As already stated, I am not a scholar of eschatological theology and my prediction of a coming apocalypse is not derived from a preconceived viewpoint. Instead, my thesis deals with measurable trends and empiric forces powerfully at work within the world system propelling us toward an ominous outcome.

By design, these trends and forces will be examined one at a time. To avoid being misled, it is advisable for the reader to refrain from making premature conclusions until all the evidence is presented. Judge each chapter on its internal merits—not on what comes before or after. Unless guided to do so, resist combining the material until we do that work together toward the end of the book. When all the pieces of the puzzle are positioned, the big picture will clarify . . . as will the implications for our collective future.

A BRIEF HISTORY OF END-TIME

The notion of the world coming to an end has been around since the world came to a beginning. Throughout the history of human awareness, life came first, followed later by death. This cycle applied not only to individuals but also to nations and empires. Tribes disappeared, languages disappeared, forests disappeared, and entire species disappeared. What's to keep the whole thing from one day just shriveling up and blowing away?

The ideas and details of end-times thought have been many and various. Although end-times thinking is often associated with

religious views, there has always been a thriving secular component to the debate as well. Astrologers and occultists also have
weighed in with their own spectacular predictions.

Whatever the source of the conviction or the perceived details
of the final event, the last several decades have seen an increased
interest in things apocalyptic. Partly such interest is related to the
turn of the millennium—an event that, after all, doesn't come along
very often. Partly it is related to the world's dramatically increased
population and the threat of pollution and climatic change. Partly
it is related to escalating global economic and political volatility.
Partly it is related to the re-emergence of statehood for Israel. But
whatever else is involved, it certainly is related to the fact that, for
the first time, we have the technological power to do the job ourselves without the help of pestilence or asteroids.

"Since 1945," notes philosopher Michael Grosso, "it began to
be technologically feasible to end life on this planet."[3] Bertrand
Russell, by all accounts possessing a brilliant mind but never a cor-
respondingly bright outlook, reflected on these technological powers
and concluded that the problem is educated man himself. "He has
survived, thitherto, through ignorance. Can he continue to survive
now that the useful degree of ignorance is lost?" Russell asked in
1961 under the shadow of very real nuclear threats.[4] "We are now
asking a narrower question than 'can man survive?' We are now asking 'can *scientific* man survive?'"[5]

SECULAR GLOOM

I have already alluded to that component of apocalyptic thought
arising from secular, scientific, and academic realms independent
of religious tradition. Let's rewind the tape 200 years and pick up
the action when Thomas Malthus struck the first salvo of modern
scientific doomsday prophecy with his publication of *Essay on the
Principle of Population*. Malthus discovered a mathematical mis-
match between the growth of population, which was geometric, and

the growth of the food supply, which was linear. Eventually, he proposed, this would lead to starvation on a mass scale. His 1798 prediction has never materialized—but never quite goes away either.

Following the Enlightenment, many in the scientific community showed a progressively declining interest in the notion of a Christian apocalypse. And after World War II—with its fifty million dead and the debut of nuclear weaponry—scientists found they no longer required God's judgment to end history. Humankind could get the job done without any help from above.

Increasingly the global community had a host of worrisome developments to lose sleep over:

World Hunger and Overpopulation—Some scientists worried about world hunger on a scale that would exceed previous human experience or imagination. With the burgeoning global population, neoMalthusianism emerged as a dominant theme. This unprecedented population explosion would be followed by widespread famine and war.

Ecocatastrophe—Other scientists despaired over threatened ecocatastrophes such as global warming, desertification, deforestation, acid rain, toxic waste, nuclear power plant accidents, ozone holes, species extinction, and resource depletion.

Infectious Disease—Still other experts worried about widespread infectious pandemics due to urban crowding, poverty, and unprecedented international travel—diseases such as AIDS, virulent influenza, a reappearance of smallpox, or the emergence of deadly new viral agents.

Weapons of Mass Destruction—Everyone, it seemed, worried about proliferating weapons of mass destruction—nuclear, chemical, and biological—whether from superpowers, rogue nations, or terrorist networks.

The warnings, complaints, and admonitions from secular scientists were voluminous, with the following but a representative sampling:

- "Human beings are getting themselves, and the rest of the world, into deeper and deeper trouble," wrote naturalist Lewis Thomas, "and I would not lay heavy odds on our survival unless we begin maturing soon."[6]
- "We may have only a few decades until Doomsday," warned astronomer Carl Sagan.[7]
- "I think human life is threatened as never before in the history of this planet," claimed nobelist Dr. George Walk, chairman of the biology department at Harvard University. "Not by one peril, but by many. They are all working together, coming to a head about the same time. And the time lies very close to the year 2000. I am one of those scientists who finds it hard to see how the human race is to bring itself much past the year 2000."[8]
- "Currently we are behaving like insane passengers on a jet plane who are busy taking all the rivets and bolts out of the craft as it flies along," writes columnist Tom Harper in the *Toronto Star.*[9]
- "We have nothing in the history of human societies that suggests that any system can be depended upon to correct itself rather than perish," explained noted anthropologist Margaret Mead.[10]

Soon, almost all futurists and scientists were hedging their bets. Alvin Toffler, for example, based *The Third Wave* (1980) predictions on what he called the "revolutionary premise." This premise "assumes that, even though the decades immediately ahead are likely to be filled with upheavals, turbulence, perhaps even widespread violence, we will not totally destroy ourselves."[11]

The acclaimed biologist E. O. Wilson was prognostically worried enough to pen an article entitled *Is Humanity Suicidal?* "Are we racing to the brink of an abyss, or are we just gathering speed for a takeoff to a wonderful future? The crystal ball is clouded; the human condition baffles all the more because it is both unprecedented and bizarre, almost beyond understanding."[12] His answer to the title question was basically "No, I hope we aren't suicidal—but I'm keeping my fingers crossed" (my construction).

Distinguished Professor Emeritus of Planning at University of Southern California, Melville C. Branch, claims that the ultimate question for humanity "is whether our species is capable of thinking and acting in its own interest to ensure its survival. Some scholars maintain that we hold within us an unconscious drive to self-destruct, which will eventually succeed." Branch believes that strategic planning is essential to avert a host of megasuicidal disasters and pandemics. And if we fail, he offers a back-up plan: "Perhaps enough genetic material could be protected for preprogrammed and undamaged robots to start up our species again for us."[13]

Bertrand Russell, however, is not even sure such genetic preservation is worth the bother. "I am writing at a dark moment (July 1961), and it is impossible to know whether the human race will last long enough for what I write to be published, or, if published, to be read," he bemoaned. "A pessimist might argue: why seek to preserve the human species? Should we not rather rejoice in the prospect of an end to the immense load of suffering and hate and fear which has hitherto darkened the life of Man?"[14]

Before leaving this discussion, perhaps it is instructive to include yet one more representation of secular thought. William Strauss and Neil Howe believe strongly in the cyclical theory of history (a belief I do not share), as described in their 1997 book, *The Fourth Turning*. They assert that every two decades modern history enters a new era—a new *turning*. The first turning is a *High*, the second an *Awakening*, the third an *Unraveling*, and the fourth a *Crisis*. This impending fourth turning is due to arrive around the year 2005. "Remnants of the old social order will disintegrate," the authors predict. "Political and economic trust will implode. Real hardship will beset the land, with severe distress that could involve questions of class, race, nation, and empire.[15]

"The next Fourth Turning could mark the end of man. It could be an omnicidal Armageddon, destroying everything, leaving nothing. If mankind ever extinguishes itself, this will probably happen when its dominant civilization triggers a Fourth Turning that ends horribly. But this end, while possible, is not likely."[16]

STRANGER THAN SCIENCE

Beyond the secular scientific end-of-the-age theories (and in some cases, *way* beyond), almost every occult, astrological, or sectarian tradition holds its own version of the apocalypse. Howard Furness claimed that earth would pass through the Oort Cloud in 2000 resulting in asteroids destroying most of the earth. Psychic Ruth Montgomery believed that, at about the same time, the earth's axis would shift causing a multitude of natural disasters—only to have enlightened people rescued by spacecraft.[17] Jehovah's Witnesses thought the end would come in 1874, then thirty years later, then 1918, 1920, 1925, 1940, 1975 . . . and finally, whenever.[18]

Edgar Cayce, before he died in 1945, formed an association that continues to promote his prophecies today. Cayce developed a reputation as *the sleeping prophet* by making prophetic utterances in a trance. His predictions include drastic world events befalling the earth between 1950 and 2000, such as earthquakes, volcanoes, and a melting of the polar caps, destroying much of California and Japan.[19]

One of the strangest and most mystical was the physician-turned-prophet Nostradamus. In 1552, this Frenchman published his master work *Centuries*, a collection of quatrains divided into 100 per century until "the end of the world in 3747."[20] His works are enjoying a resurgent popularity today, and he is credited with having foreseen AIDS, communism, and nuclear weapons. Some of his most dramatic predictions were directed at the turn of the millennium:

> In the year 1999 and seven months
> The great King of Terror will come from the sky.

> He will bring back to life the great king of the
> Mongols.
> Before and after war reigns happily unrestrained.

Although he did not predict world annihilation in 1999, he did predict great war, famine, pestilence, and despair.[21]

THE CHRISTIAN APOCALYPSE

The Christian version of end-times prophecy has perhaps garnered the most attention and generated the most enthusiasm. Even though Jesus warned against setting specific dates for His return,[22] He nevertheless admonished his followers to recognize the signs of its approach. In that spirit, Christians throughout the last two thousand years often have felt convinced of sufficient evidence to believe theirs might indeed represent the last generation. Martin Luther's theology was strongly eschatological, for example, and he believed the world would end within a hundred years. Luther, according to the Reformation scholar Heiko Oberman, "was proclaiming the Last Days, not the modern age."[23]

Most Christian eschatology can be divided into three categories: *a*millennialism, *post*millennialism, and *pre*millennialism. These categories differ in how they view the biblical concept of the Millennium (1,000 years) in Revelation 20.

The *amillennialists* do not believe in a literal thousand-year reign of Christ on the earth. Instead, they believe the current Church Age will be followed by a general resurrection, judgment, and a new heaven and earth. The *postmillennialists* believe that a golden age of progressive righteousness and a thousand years of peace will be followed by the return of Christ, thus terminating history. This perspective is not apocalyptic. The *premillennialists* believe that Christ will return literally to earth before He establishes the thousand-year reign. In this view, there are two dramatic occurrences that will predate the return of Christ:

- A sudden disappearance of all believers called the *rapture*
- A seven-year period of global anguish called the *tribulation*

The premillennialist view contains a strong expectation for many cataclysmic events in the end times. The most popular form of premillennialism today is called dispensationalism, which teaches that God divides human history into distinct eras. Currently, according to this teaching, we are living in the Church Age.

While I am not theologically competent to make a confident determination about which millennial viewpoint is most biblically accurate, my independent research does indicate that apocalyptic events await us. Again, let me emphasize that this book is not a theological treatise but instead a trends-based estimation of our most probable future. Based on that research, I believe there is abundant and compelling evidence to suggest the world system is approaching a cataclysmic conclusion.

I can't tell the world system what to do, any more than I can tell God what to do. I can't manipulate the future to suit my suppositions. All I can do is put myself in the vicinity of the truth and then hope to understand the evidence encountered. This requires both intellectual and spiritual integrity. We should never be guilty of "cooking the data" to prove our biases. On the other hand, neither should we be so narrow in our theological prejudices or so stubborn in our scientific preconceptions that we fail to acknowledge the future forces chasing us with sticks of dynamite.

THE CURTAIN CALL

In the remainder of this book I will detail trend lines that are simultaneously fascinating and worrisome. If this evidence happens to correspond with God's plan for the final curtain, it simply means we have been picked to live in a most remarkable age. Should Jesus choose to return on our shift, He would certainly upset many people and disrupt lots of plans. But then, He is the Lord and has a right to do what He wants.

"The doctrine of the Second Coming is deeply uncongenial to the whole evolutionary or developmental character of modern thought," wrote C. S. Lewis in *The World's Last Night*. "We have been taught to think of the world as something that grows slowly towards perfection, something that 'progresses' or 'evolves.' Christian Apocalyptic offers us no such hope. It does not even foretell (which would be more tolerable to our habits of thought) a gradual decay. It foretells a sudden, violent end imposed from without . . . a curtain rung down on the play—'Halt!'"[24]

Evidently, a majority of Americans agree with Lewis (always a wise theological position to adopt). In a recent poll, fully two-thirds of Americans believe that Christ will return to earth someday. This belief is even found in one-out-of-every-three people who never attend church.[25] In a separate poll, sixty percent indicate a belief that the world will end, and a third expect this culmination in the near future.[26] If so many of us believe it is coming, why do so few of us prepare?

Jesus understood the preoccupation He would find upon His return. "Just as it was in the days of Noah," He explained, "so also will it be in the days of the Son of Man. People were eating, drinking, marrying and being given in marriage up to the day Noah entered the ark. Then the flood came and destroyed them all. It was the same in the days of Lot. People were eating and drinking, buying and selling, planting and building. But the day Lot left Sodom, fire and sulfur rained down from heaven and destroyed them all. It will be just like this on the day the Son of Man is revealed."[27]

His words sound dramatic, even dreadful. Is fear, then, to be our response? Fear of Noah's flood, or of Lot's fire? Fear of the end? . . . of the Son? No—not unless we have something to fear. The best way, and the only way, to live without fear is to live ready. Whenever the end comes, however it comes, be ready for it. And there is more to being ready than eating and drinking, buying and selling, planting and building. "Precisely because we cannot predict the moment," advised Lewis, "we must be ready at all moments."[28]

If God has called us for such a time as this, He has His reasons. His message is the only hope, and He has asked us to bear that word to the hopeless. His foundation is the only place to stand. His love is the only force that can endure the fire of the future.

If God has chosen this to be a special time, why did He pick you? Why did He pick me? Why did He pick our generational shift for these remarkable and unprecedented conditions? I am not sure. But let's understand it is a privilege, and let's live ready.

As perhaps a first step in the readying process, let me now take you on a guided tour of the trends and forces that are hurtling us irreversibly toward oblivion.

CHAPTER TWO

PROFUSION THROUGH PROGRESS

Imagine two CNN reporters approaching your house to conduct an interview. The topic under investigation concerns the many changes in our modern world. In the midst of the interview, they ask the following question: "If you could use only *one word* to describe all that is happening in the world, which word would you choose?"

If such a question were put to me, many possible choices would present themselves. But a word that would be high on my list—and possibly at the top of the list—would be the word *more*.

No matter where we look—it makes no difference—there is always *more*. No matter what topic we consider—it makes no difference—there is always *more*.

Obviously there are more people—lots more people.

There are more cars traveling more miles over more roads, and more airplanes carrying more passengers on more flights. There are more televisions broadcasting more programs over more stations. There are more computers, more books, and more magazines, all processing and distributing more information—lots more information.

There are more businesses offering more services and making more products—lots more products. There are more buildings, more restaurants, more medications, more telephones, and more money. Lots more money.

There are more activities and commitments, more choices and decisions, more change and stress, more technology and complexity.

There is, in short, more . . . of everything. Wherever we look, we are surrounded by more. Always.

EVERYTHING GROWS

Thirty years ago, systems engineer Roberto Vacca had already accurately characterized this trend by observing: "Everything grows: everything is on the increase, and every year the speed of that increase is greater."[1]

I doubt that you need much substantiation for his assertion, but for the sake of completeness consider the following:

- In 1800 there were *one* billion people; in 1930, *two* billion; 1960, *three* billion; 1975, *four* billion; 1987, *five* billion; and 1998, *six* billion.
- Life expectancy worldwide was 21 years at the time of Christ; 48 years in 1955; and 65 years in 1995. This is expected to rise to 85 years by 2050.[2,3]
- Global food production has tripled since World War II, outpacing even population growth.
- We use seven times as much water as in 1900.[4]
- Paper consumption per capita in the United States tripled from 1940 to 1980, and tripled again in the next ten years (to 1,800 pounds).[5]
- There are 62,000 new book titles and new editions each year.

- There are 1,005 typeface fonts available at one store.
- In 1960, the average CEO traveled 12,000 miles a year. Today, the average CEO travels 112,000 miles a year.[6]
- Every year, fifty quadrillion transistors are produced, more than six million for every human on the planet.[7]
- The Physician Desk Reference (PDR) had 300 pages when it first came out in 1948; fifty years later it has 3,000 pages.
- The NBA rulebook had two pages when basketball first started a hundred years ago; it now has 114 pages.
- In 1975, there were 3,000 international nongovernment organizations (NGOs) in every field, from ceramics and metallurgy to religion and sports. Today, there are over 25,000.[8]
- In 1978 the average grocery store had 11,000 products; now it has 30,000 products.
- There are 550 different kinds of coffee, 250 different kinds of toothpaste, and 175 different kinds of salad dressing.
- There are 2,500 different types of light bulbs—in one store alone.

It has been predicted that in the next twenty-five years, the total world production will double.[9] *More* has been busy, and we have come to expect nothing less.

THE NORMALIZATION OF *MORE*

Having become so accustomed to accepting this state of affairs as normal, we seldom stop to think about it. It doesn't even occur to us to ask: *Why is this happening? Where is all this* "more" *coming from?*

As a matter of fact, always having *more* is such an accepted part of life that not having *more* would be regarded as abnormal. Not only is it normal to have more, but it is also widely regarded as desirable. Our strong preference is to have more. The people who do not have more feel deprived, perhaps even victimized.

The phenomenon of *more* I call profusion. That we are surrounded by a powerful flood of profusion is so elementary we seldom stop to think about it. But I am going to ask us to think about it—deeply—because it is part of my empiric argument for the end of the age.

PROFUSION FROM PROGRESS

If *more* comes from *profusion*, where does profusion come from? There are several modern forces that contribute to the phenomenon of profusion—but mostly it comes from progress. Wherever progress is most active, profusion is most active. Often, without even realizing it, we measure progress by measuring profusion. We can even say that profusion is a function of progress. Let me explain.

Modern people, generally speaking, believe in progress. We have faith in progress and we applaud it. Progress is widely regarded as a good thing. Developed countries are proud of their progress, while developing countries are trying to get in on it.

But what exactly is progress? How does it work? To answer the first question: Progress is the notion that life continually improves. To answer the second question: Progress works largely through the processes of differentiation and proliferation. Because progress differentiates our universe, it always gives us *more and more of everything faster and faster*. And because progress proliferates whatever it creates, it always gives us *more and more of everything cheaper and cheaper.*

Differentiation—Let's take first the case of differentiation. Differentiation is the process of proceeding from the general to the specific, from the simple to the complex, from the one to the many. It is a developmental process perhaps most easily understood through illustration. If, for example, we give progress a piece of cloth, it will use that material to make various articles of clothing. First, perhaps, a shirt. Then a blouse. Then a pair of pants and a skirt. Then handkerchiefs, gloves, and perhaps a hat. This is differentiating the cloth.

Proliferation—Next, let's take the fairly obvious case of proliferation. Once progress has differentiated the material and made many different articles of clothing, then it proliferates each article of clothing making as many copies as the market will bear.

Throw in the powerful cofactors of technology and money, and the engines of progress will put on a dizzying performance, differentiating and proliferating twenty-four hours a day, 365 days a year on a global scale. As a result, progress and the conditions of modern day living have given us more and more of everything faster and faster.

It is profusion in abundance. And progress is very good at making it happen.

UNMEASURABLE

Profusion is such a profound force in defining our present and determining our future that if we are to fully understand our world environment it is essential that we first understand profusion in all its magnitude. There is only one problem—fully comprehending profusion is not possible.

Allow me to clarify. It is possible to grasp the *concept* of profusion, defined as the generalized phenomenon of *more*: more people, more progress, more products, and more of everything else you can think of, all added together. But the *mathematical physical reality* of profusion is simply too large and inclusive to grasp.

This presents us with a special difficulty. If we do not completely grasp both the *concept* and the *mathematical physical reality* of global profusion, we also will fail to completely grasp the powerful dynamics of our world system. Additionally, we will put ourselves at risk of underestimating the implications of the thesis outlined in this book. Therefore, it is important that we expand our thinking as broadly as possible, and having done so, to still mistrust our abilities to perceive it all.

Let us return again to the realm of medicine for the purposes of illustration. There are perhaps similarities in trying to understand profusion and trying to understand the human body. When I taught orientation classes in our residency program at the University of Wisconsin medical school, I would tell the young doctors that no physician ever understood the human body. There are 10^{27} atoms in the body, ninety percent of which turn over every year. In each human body, one trillion trillion atoms turn over and become new atoms every hour. We each have sixty thousand miles of blood vessels. We make ten million red blood cells every second. The number of nonlinear differential equations that the retina of the eye must solve in one-third of a second would take a Cray supercomputer one hundred years to solve. The truth is, the human body is staggeringly incomprehensible.

While we can understand the *concept* of a human body, it is not possible for us to grasp the *mathematical realities* involved. We simply are not capable of comprehension at such a level. Similarly, in the area of profusion, the mathematical realities are of an order of magnitude beyond which our brains will take us.

Let me make the following assertions to demonstrate how large a concept we are dealing with and how hard it is to fully comprehend.

- Profusion is virtually unmeasurable. First, there are no units to use. Second, it would be impossible to collect all the data. Third, it changes and grows so fast that it is always a moving target traveling at, shall we say, the speed of light.
- Profusion has no common frame of reference. Because it is so large, is growing so fast, and is virtually unmeasurable, we have nothing in our daily existence with which to compare it.
- Profusion is always underestimated. Humans will always remain behind the curve in our understanding of

profusion—a point that will be further developed in the
chapter on exponentiality.

- Profusion is deceptively complex. Because we think it is a
rather simple and generic concept, the temptation is to
believe that we can get our minds around profusion. Such
a false feeling of security only misleads us even further.
Even when we feel we are being definitive in our understanding of profusion, we are still leaving something out.
We will forget to count bowling balls. Or receipts from
department stores. Or each piece of corn grown in
India . . . or each satellite orbiting . . . or each satellite
dish . . . or each television program coming over each
satellite dish. We will forget each R&D experiment, each
line of each IRS form, each toothpick, and each toggle
switch in each space craft (John Glenn had 56 toggle
switches in his first craft in 1962 and 856 in his second
craft in 1998. Don't forget to increase your profusion
number to include this increase!).

Let me introduce one additional fact about global profusion
that will be explored more fully in the following chapter. Profusion
only goes in one direction: up. The rare exceptions to this rule are
localized and temporary. Of course there will be decreases in the *rate
of growth* of profusion, but it is important to notice that *this is not
the same as profusion itself decreasing.*

Profusion is, in one way of looking at it, a kind of enormous
global pile. And each year, more is added on top of last year's pile.
The pile itself does not go away—it just keeps growing larger,
layer after layer after layer.

Take, for example, the case of automobiles. For purposes of
illustration, let's say that there are one million new automobiles
sold this year in the United States. If next year there is a recession,
perhaps there will only be 800,000 sold rather than one million.
Some who are not careful would assert that this means profusion is

decreasing. But think twice—the *rate* of profusion might have decreased, but profusion in fact continued to increase. Notice that there are now 800,000 more cars than there were the year before. This number must be added to the previous number that existed the year before, thereby increasing profusion. (In fact, the number of registered cars in the United States has increased nearly fourfold since 1950.)

Historically speaking, profusion climbs inexorably. Perhaps we might best think of profusion as sitting atop a huge rocket blasting straight up, burning a billion tons of rocket fuel per second. If this illustration sounds like an exaggeration to you, then you still do not completely comprehend the *mathematical physical reality* of profusion.

"A SPECIAL MOMENT IN HISTORY"

All of this makes for a unique, unprecedented historical experience. "We may live in the strangest, most thoroughly different moment since human beings took up farming . . ." explains Bill McKibben in his fascinating and provocative *Atlantic Monthly* cover article "A Special Moment in History." "Since then, time has flowed in one direction—toward *more*, which we have taken to be progress. At first the momentum was gradual, almost imperceptible, checked by wars and the Dark Ages and plagues and taboos; but in recent centuries it has accelerated, the curve of every graph steepening like the Himalayas rising from the Asian steppe. We have climbed quite high. Of course, fifty years ago one could have said the same thing, and fifty years before that, and fifty years before *that*. But in each case it could have been premature. We've increased the population fourfold in that 150 years; the amount of food we grow has gone up faster still; the size of our economy has quite simply exploded.

"But now," he concludes, "now may be the special time."[10]

I do not agree with all of Mr. McKibben's assertions in this article. But I certainly agree that this is a "special moment in history."

Never before has the world system seen six billion people living together — heading for ten billion. Never before have we seen such speed and such power as we have available today. Never before have we seen such complexity, and never before has the complexity been this tightly coupled.

Never before have we seen such profusion. The truth is, we do not know for sure what will happen next, for we have never been here before. But there is good reason to be worried.

CHAPTER THREE

THE IRREVERSIBILITY OF PROGRESS

The phenomenon of profusion is irreversible, primarily because progress is a one-way street. The original engineers, it seems, forgot to install a reverse gear. As a result, for a multitude of reasons, the process of modernization is unidirectional. There is no turning back.

Regarding this irreversibility, progress can't help itself. It has only been taught to go in one direction — differentiation — thus always giving us more and more of everything faster and faster. This is precisely what we have asked and expected of progress. Who in their right mind would expect progress to give us *less and less, slower and slower*?

"The society is caught up in a dynamic of change which no power can stop," explained economics professor Kenneth Boulding in 1964. "Now that the transition is under way, there is no going back on it."[1] Sociologist Alvin Toffler agreed. "We cannot and must not turn off the switch of technological progress," he wrote in 1970. "To turn our back on technology would be not only stupid but immoral."[2]

In 1976, respected futurist Herman Kahn offered similar sentiments: "Any concerted attempt to stop or even slow 'progress' appreciably . . . is catastrophe-prone. At the minimum, it would probably require the creation of extraordinarily repressive governments or movements— and probably a repressive international system."[3] These words were but early indicators of what has only been echoed more forcibly each new year by each new futurist thinker: History flows only in the direction of technological progress.

That the entire world system will therefore experience an ever-escalating profusion is, of course, not perceived as bad news. Quite the opposite, it is precisely what is universally hoped for, sought after, and expected. It would even be accurate to state that if such a profusion *failed* to materialize, we would have billions of bitterly disappointed people.

POWERFULLY PROFICIENT PROGRESS

Progress is powerful. It has shown a remarkable ability to pile millions, even billions, of people on its back and still go uphill. Progress has grown so flush with power and success that it now often operates under an autonomous strength and speed.

Because progress has proven so alluringly proficient, we have decided to build our entire economy around its twin engines of differentiation and proliferation. We have hitched our wagon to that star and progress has delivered on a grandiose scale, leaving us both gratified and awed. As a result, our way of life is predicated upon the growth that progress brings. Therefore, if we were to stop growing, both our economy and our way of life would collapse. This is not a particularly popular option and to date has not made it onto the platform of any major political party.

To continue in the direction we are going is our only apparent option. Even if we wanted to stop, slow down, or change direction, we would not know how to do so. But it's all a moot point anyway, because who in their right mind wants to stop?

There are at least three reasons why our current path to progress—leading to inevitably increasing profusion—is irreversible.

- First, the performance of our economy is completely dependent on progress continuing in its current direction. And the economy always gets whatever it needs. Thus we cannot go backward because the economy will throw an unbearable tantrum, and we will do anything to prevent that.
- Second, we are habituated to the lifestyle progress provides. One might even say, with frightening accuracy, that we are addicted. Thus we cannot go backward because we cannot kick the progress habit.
- Third, each new level of progress not only supersedes the former, but supplants it. It annihilates it. The former no longer exists. Thus we can't go backward because there is no pre-progress state to return to.

Let's examine each of these three reasons in more detail.

THE PREEMINENCE OF THE ECONOMY

When first undertaking a thorough study of society nearly twenty years ago, I began reading everything in sight (aided by my wife, Linda, a tireless researcher). Over a period of five years, I carefully assembled (figuratively speaking) a cultural jigsaw puzzle with 50,000 pieces. After I had assembled the entire puzzle, interlocking and integrating each piece, I stood back to take it all in. The purpose: to see and understand clearly the big picture.

Next I took the pieces of the puzzle and mentally made them into a 50,000 piece mobile. After assembling the entire mobile, I pulled on each piece to see how the entire mobile would react. The purpose: to see how each piece was connected to each of the other pieces.

I then began the process of identifying trends one-by-one, always looking for new connections, new insights, new synthesizing perspectives. Despite my success in identifying fifty such cultural trends, still I scratched my head looking for a grand unifying theory. What was causing society to go in the direction it was going? Where were these trends and forces coming from? What was the most powerful influence? Why was all this happening as it was, and why was it all happening now?

When the role of progress clarified itself in my thinking, it quickly moved to the head of the class. Clearly, progress was a powerful, almost unstoppable force. Still, there was something I was not seeing. What was it? Finally the light went on. It was so elementary that I am almost embarrassed to discuss it publicly. The answer: economics. Economics was *the* dominant force. It was preeminent. Economics, linked as it was to progress, ruled.

The concept of economics has only been around for about five hundred years, and as a scientific discipline, the field of classical economics is a mere two hundred years old. Its rapid ascent to dominance has surprised even economists. In sheer power and influence, economics now dwarfs all other forces in modern society. It has been fully canonized as the new sacred domain.

As we have already seen, our economic system is designed to work through the mechanism of progress with its twin engines of differentiation and proliferation. If somehow progress were to slow, our economy would slow. If progress were to stop, our economy would stop. If progress were to reverse—giving us less and less, slower and slower—our entire economy would fall apart. With it, our vaunted way of life would disappear.

In a tug of war, the economy wins. The economy *always* wins. And because progress and the economy are directly related, progress is not going to slow down. We can count on *more and more of everything faster and faster* from here on out because the economy requires it. Profusion will continue unabated, precisely because it is necessary for our economy. And the economy wins all debates. The first rule of modernity: Always give the economy whatever it wants. It is not a rule I always agree with. But then, I am not in charge.

Questions naturally arise, especially when considering the historical and global perspectives. What about economic recession or depression? What about countries with corrupt and oppressive governments? What about the Third World experience where little or no progress exists? What about historical periods such as the Dark Ages? Aren't these exceptions? Not at all. In fact, such illustrations actually support the point I am attempting to make.

An economic recession or depression obviously is not the preferred condition for any society. Therefore, people and systems will work strenuously to return to the preferred condition of progress and economic prosperity, thus forcefully leading to enhanced profusion. If we examine the history of human societies over the past two hundred years, each recession or depression was temporary, was resisted, and was eventually overcome by the process of progress. Thus profusion was put back on track.

What about corrupt or oppressive governments? Again, powerful social forces arise to resist this condition. If we were to ask people living under such conditions whether they prefer corruption and oppression or freedom and prosperity, one hundred percent would favor some form of freedom and prosperity (although not all would favor the capitalist system). Eventually, these people will exert their collective will to restore the preferred state, thus enhancing profusion.

What about poor and destitute Third World countries? Such countries, despite their immense difficulties, nevertheless experience ever-increasing profusion: more people living in more houses, eating more food, and consuming more products. Simply travel to a crowded city in such a country and observe the teeming hoards of people. What we observe is a measure of increased profusion.

What about reaching back to distant history, such as the Dark Ages? The experience of the Dark Ages is not binding in this context, for it predates progress. The modern era of progress is best considered to be perhaps 200 or 300 years old. And during that span, progress has been relentless—and irreversible.

One additional point needs to be made. Even with temporary and regional hardships such as discussed above, still total profusion *slows but does not reverse.* Take, for example, the case of modern China. The government is oppressive and the people are poor. Nevertheless, profusion has dramatically increased with increasing population, buildings, products, and now the mainstreamed and accepted push for increased economic well-being.

For total profusion to reverse would require the deaths of billions of people and the leveling of vast tracts of the socioeconomic landscape—destruction of houses, possessions, stores, factories, and other property on almost a continental scale. There is simply no historical precedent for such occurrences.

OUR HABITUATION AND ADDICTION TO PROGRESS

Another reason progress is a one-way street is because of human dependence. Our dependence on progress—and thus profusion as well—is the type of behavior that can be called refractory, even addictive. It is my contention that we have developed lifestyles so completely habituated to progress that even if serious ill effects were proven, we would still find it very difficult to modify our lifestyles in any kind of substantive way.

We know in medicine that it is frustratingly difficult for people to change their behaviors. Most poor health is the result of poor health habits. If unhealthy people could change these habits, disorders such as obesity, deconditioning from poor exercise, stress, sleep disorders, and many emotional illnesses would be easier to treat, to say nothing of the problems related to drugs, smoking, gambling, pornography, and abuse.

Even issues related to having a good marriage and wise parenting could often be fairly easily solved if people would agree to abide by a few basic fundamental principles. But it is naive to think this is going to happen in a simplistic way. Anyone who has worked in the people-helping fields knows just how refractory human behavior is. Pastors, therapists, and nutritionists, for example, realize how much easier it would make their work if people would just change those habits that are causing problems. Yet it happens slowly at best, and often not at all.

It is possible to carry this discussion beyond habituation to the related issue of addiction. Part of my assertion that progress is irreversible is based on the contention that we are addicted to progress and therefore are quite willing to accept whatever profusion comes our way—even should it prove harmful. In that sense, progress needs to be added to the long list of addictive agents. It was not at first apparent this would be the case, but honest reflection now reveals a clear addictive effect.

One of the best ways to assess addiction is to take the substance in question away and watch for signs of withdrawal. Consider, for example, television. How many people could abandon their televisions—even if they were thoroughly convinced it would be strongly beneficial to do so? Would it be difficult to give it up? Yes. Would there be withdrawal? Of course. Be sure you are interacting with this illustration at the level I am asking. I am *not* asking whether you believe it is culturally beneficial to give up televisions. I am only asking *could we as a culture do it*? The answer is no.

Beyond television, think additionally of American society voluntarily giving up shopping, movies, popular music, telephones, air conditioning, automobiles, eating out, professional sports, and access to health care. The probability of such happening—even if we were convinced of its necessity—is about the same as the probability of Donald Trump moving into a tarpaper hut. If even McDonalds and the NFL were taken away, half of our society would collapse within a month.

Lifestyle is powerful. We must account for the fact that much of it is unhealthy but we still don't do anything about it. The models of habituation and addiction serve well as explanations. If we are habituated, even addicted, then should progress and profusion present a problem, our level of dependency would make it very hard for us to reverse direction.

RETENTION OF ALL PREVIOUS KNOWLEDGE AND EXPERIENCE

The third piece of evidence demonstrating the irreversibility principle has to do with what we might call the *involuntary retention* problem (not to be confused with a urological condition).

All of life's experiences—that which has been known or discovered, that which has been printed, that which has been seen or heard—are involuntarily preserved on our collective unerasable memory bank. We have a *noteworthy* inability to purge from our collective memory that which is *useless.* More significantly, we have a *frightening* inability to purge from our collective memory that which is *harmful.*

Once Published—Once something has been *published,* it cannot be *unpublished.* Once something finds its way into print it has forever entered the public domain and cannot be removed. Even if we tried to recall the message or print a correction or issue a retraction, the message cannot be successfully forgotten. There is no delete button for the world's memory. As has been said thousands of times following the printed correction, "But who do I see to get my reputation back?" Explains former Librarian of Congress Daniel Boorstin, "Once the printing press had done its work, there was no force on earth, no law or edict, that could retrieve the message."[4] Yes, you can perhaps *correct* the original message, but the point is, you cannot *erase* it. *Publishing is irreversible.*

Once Seen—Once something has been *seen* it cannot be *unseen.* For example, once advertisers flash sensuous images across the screen, these images cannot intentionally be forgotten (as the advertisers well know). Once the blood-splattered scenes of a modern slasher movie roll across your sight, they will live on in the screen of the mind. Forever. You have no volitional control over forgetting. *Seeing is irreversible.*

Once Heard—Once something has been *heard* it cannot be *unheard.* The rapid dissemination of terrifying criminal stories frighten children hundreds of miles from the scene of the violence. Once these audible impressions implant, it is impossible to intentionally erase them. *Hearing is irreversible.*

Once Known—Once something is *known* it cannot be *unknown.* If we become aware that a sitting president is guilty of sexual indiscretions, it is impossible to return to a national state of mind where this is *unknown.* Once someone tells you a rumor in church or at work, you cannot unknow it. Once broadcast, it cannot be erased. *Knowing is irreversible.*

Once Discovered—Once something has been *discovered* it cannot be *undiscovered.* The world would presumably be safer if nuclear weapons had never been developed. Now, however, it is impossible to expunge from the memory of the world how to construct them. The 1998 nuclear explosions by India and Pakistan suddenly and starkly reminded the international community of this destabilizing truth. *Discovering is irreversible.*

"The growth of knowledge is one of the most irreversible forces known to mankind," explains Boulding. "It takes a catastrophe of very large dimensions to diminish the total stock of knowledge in the possession of man. Even in the rise and fall of great civilizations, surprisingly little has been permanently lost, and much that was lost for a short time was easily regained. Hence there is no hope for ignorance or for a morality based on it."[5]

If only we could learn how to unlearn. If only we knew how to forget! "In a century when the stock of human knowledge and of collective memories would be multiplied, recorded, and diffused as never before," observes Boorstin, "forgetting would become more than ever a prerequisite for sanity."[6] But once an experience is public—once it is published, seen, heard, known, or discovered—it remains forever. Now we must deal with it. At best, it is information pollution, a kind of static that clogs our memory systems. At worst, it is ruinous to our societal health. In our modern age, true innocence is a fragile state indeed.

The irreversibility implications are clear. Once progress has reached a certain rung on the ladder, we can't slip back into a more primitive innocent state even if we want to. Once we *print* it, *see* it, *hear* it, *discover* it, or *know* it—we are stuck with it. For good or ill. As the saying goes, you can't put the genie back into the bottle. Genie escapage is an irreversible phenomenon; progress and its accompanying profusion are likewise irreversible for the same reasons.

Science and technology now realize that once they climb to a higher rung on the ladder of progress, the rung underneath falls away. It is possible to keep going up, but impossible to come back down. Whether we view ignorance as destitution or bliss makes no difference—the bridge back to it is burned. Once people discovered knives, it was impossible to get them to fight just with hands. And once people discovered gunpowder, it was impossible to get them to fight just with knives. And once people discovered the atom, it has proven a dicey proposition to convince them to fight just with gunpowder.

REGRESS?

Some who read this chapter might think it is one big rhetorical question, for who would *want* progress and profusion to reverse even if they could? Beyond these three binding reasons why progress is unidirectional, who in their right mind would *want* to reverse progress anyway? We have a name for progress in reverse—it is called regress. And the use of this word is always pejorative.

The truth of the matter is, we have no desire to change. We are content to be on this road of more and more, faster and faster. We actively prefer the path of profusion. And we have no intention of going in the opposite direction.

But my point is this: yes, perhaps we prefer it this way. But if progress and profusion later prove to be a problem, could we throw the entire thing into reverse and simply back it all up? The answer is "No." Involuntary retention will not allow it. Our habituation and addiction will not allow it. And most assuredly, the economy will never allow it.

There is no empiric evidence to suggest that progress can or will reverse itself. There is no historic evidence to suggest that progress can or will reverse itself. There is no common sense evidence to suggest that progress can or will reverse itself.

Profusion is a one-way street, flowing only in the increasing direction.

CHAPTER FOUR

THE PHENOMENON OF EXPONENTIAL GROWTH

People today are well aware of chain reactions. They know that chain reactions—such as nuclear fission, global economics, or hamster reproduction—are fascinating and make interesting movies. They also intuitively realize that if uncontrolled, chain reactions can be both volatile and dangerous. What people don't know about chain reactions is, historically speaking, we are living in the middle of one.

Progress is a powerful process. It is also a highly desirable process the world around. As we have seen, it works by differentiation and proliferation, thus inevitably and irreversibly resulting in more and more of everything faster and faster. Under current conditions this differentiation almost always happens rapidly, and many times even exponentially. As a result, many contemporary processes not only grow, they *explode*. Because little in our day-to-day lives happens exponentially, however, our natural tendency is to underestimate what this means and to undercalculate how extraordinarily this type of change occurs.

Let's bring in some historical perspective. For nearly the entire duration of human history, change was slow and measurable. Life happened minute by minute, hour by hour, day by day, year by year. Thus, perhaps, have Shakespeare's sentiments rung true for the inhabitants of every generation: "Tomorrow, and tomorrow, and tomorrow, creeps in this petty pace from day to day to the last syllable of recorded time." Because of this, our customary experience is to think linearly, to plan according to the confines of a linear paradigm, to view our lives as a beginning-to-end straight line.

Now, however, something dramatic has happened. Something different is going down on our generational shift. The fundamentals have changed. Life pace and change are escalating wildly. Without our permission, history has picked up speed, turbo-charged by progress. Add in the powerful cofactors of technology and information, mix it with abundant economic "gunpowder," and you have cooked yourself up a nice cocktail of exponential explosiveness. The locomotive guiding history jumped the tracks, and instead of traveling down the local-stop commuter spur, it switched to supersonic status. Instead of chugging, it now explodes out of the station, breaking the sound barrier before it even leaves the gate.

As a result, much in our world experience is now happening exponentially. The emergence of exponentiality is new and its significance is incalculable. Yet most people, not knowing how to think in exponential terms, consistently underestimate it.

The graphs on the following pages serve to demonstrate how widespread the phenomenon of exponentiality is within both our national and global systems.

MOON SHOT

Let's compare linear and exponential by looking at the math involved. To illustrate, let me give you a quiz. (For those who are already familiar with this illustration, stick with it—there is something new for you as well.) Take a piece of paper and fold it in half

LIFE EXPECTANCY

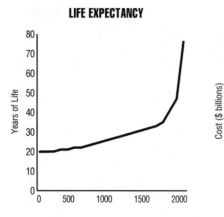

HEALTH CARE EXPENDITURES (U.S.)

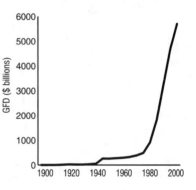

GROSS DOMESTIC PRODUCT (U.S.)

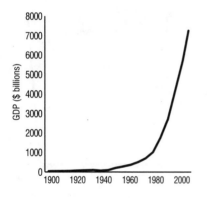

GROSS FEDERAL DEBT (U.S.)

AIR MILES TRAVELED

(Scheduled, U.S. Airline Industry, Domestic and Foreign)

VOLUME OF ADVERTISING

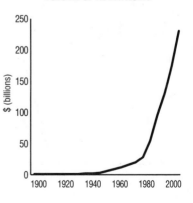

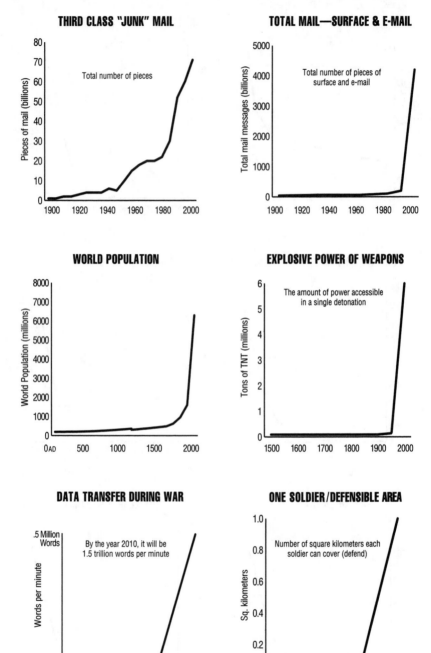

THIRD CLASS "JUNK" MAIL

Pieces of mail (billions)

Total number of pieces

80 · 70 · 60 · 50 · 40 · 30 · 20 · 10 · 0

1900 · 1920 · 1940 · 1960 · 1980 · 2000

TOTAL MAIL—SURFACE & E-MAIL

Total mail messages (billions)

Total number of pieces of surface and e-mail

5000 · 4000 · 3000 · 2000 · 1000 · 0

1900 · 1920 · 1940 · 1960 · 1980 · 2000

WORLD POPULATION

World Population (millions)

8000 · 7000 · 6000 · 5000 · 4000 · 3000 · 2000 · 1000 · 0

0 AD · 500 · 1000 · 1500 · 2000

EXPLOSIVE POWER OF WEAPONS

Tons of TNT (millions)

The amount of power accessible in a single detonation

6 · 5 · 4 · 3 · 2 · 1 · 0

1500 · 1600 · 1700 · 1800 · 1900 · 2000

DATA TRANSFER DURING WAR

Words per minute

.5 Million Words

By the year 2010, it will be 1.5 trillion words per minute

30 Words

1850 · 1900 · 1950 · 2000

ONE SOLDIER/DEFENSIBLE AREA

Sq. kilometers

Number of square kilometers each soldier can cover (defend)

1.0 · 0.8 · 0.6 · 0.4 · 0.2 · 0.0

1850 · 1900 · 1950 · 2000

forty times. How thick is it? Answer: It would go from here to the moon. Most people have great difficulty grasping this, and well they should. It sounds unbelievable. But the math is correct.

Let's push the illustration a bit further. Double this piece of paper another forty times. Now how thick is it? Answer: It reaches halfway across the Milky Way Galaxy. Let's keep going and double it twenty more times. With the paper folded a total of one hundred times, how thick is it? Answer: It would extend to the far wall of the universe.

Now let's factor in one more dimension: time. It takes three seconds to fold a standard piece of paper in half. At such a rate, theoretically we can fold this paper one hundred times in five minutes. Therefore, in the next five minutes, we can fold a piece of paper in half one hundred times, thus extending to the far wall of the universe. Welcome to the unbelievable world of exponentiality!

A HISTORY OF EXPONENTIAL THOUGHT

I am not the first to bring up the issue of exponentiality. I also am not invoking its use in exactly the same manner as those before me. Futurists and alarmists have been examining the effects of exponential change for several decades. Initially the major concern was applied to such standard doomsday discussion as over-population, energy consumption, resource depletion, and environmental pollution.

My use of exponentiality will be on a somewhat different track. But before I reveal to you my intention regarding the exponential effect, it might be helpful to review a sampling of the early literature on this matter.

1968—**Paul Ehrlich** was an early and high-decibel entrant to the debate with his controversial best-seller *The Population Bomb*. Ehrlich, a Stanford biologist, pointed out that population was growing exponentially. If left unchecked for the next 900 years, this would lead to 60,000,000,000,000,000 (sixty million billion) people on the face of the earth.[1] "The causal chain of the deterioration is easily followed to its source. Too many cars, too many factories, too much detergent, too much pesticide, multiplying contrails, inadequate sewage treatment plants, too little water, too much carbon dioxide—all can be traced easily to *too many people*."[2] He advocated strict population control and his ominous conclusion: "It is certainly clear that if population growth proceeds much further the probabilities of wars will be immensely increased."[3]

1971—**Richard Falk,** Princeton professor of international law, warned in *This Endangered Planet* that "the human race has between ten and a hundred years left to fashion a response to a situation of growing danger . . . provoked by the explosion of people and technology past the point of overload."[4] Humankind, Falk maintained, is passing through the early stages of its first planetary crisis. "The interrelated dimensions of this crisis are population pressure, multiple forms of pollution, resource depletion, and the danger of wars of mass destruction. It is the technological character of contemporary society that gives the planetary crisis its apocalyptic character."[5] The technology is too powerful, the change is too fast, the systems are too unstable, and the math is too threatening. "Underlying the entire discussion is the validity of a certain amount of exponential thinking—that is, worrying about the future because of trends and rates of changes in the present," observed Falk.[6]

1972—**Dennis Meadows,** et al., in filing the first report of The Club of Rome, struck perhaps the loudest salvo to date with *The Limits to Growth.* In it the authors dealt extensively with exponentiality and its ominous implications for the entire world system. "Nearly all of mankind's current activities, from use of fertilizer to expansion of cites, can be represented by exponential growth curves."[7] Additionally, "Virtually every pollutant that has been measured as a function of time appears to be increasing exponentially."[8] After warning against the dangers of overly imaginative technological optimism, the authors conclude: "Every day of continued exponential growth brings the world system closer to the ultimate limits to that growth. A decision to do nothing is a decision to increase the risk of collapse. . . . We suspect on the basis of present knowledge of the physical constraints of the planet that the growth phase cannot continue for another one hundred years."[9]

1972—Jay Forrester, M.I.T. professor and one of the first to develop computer models to study the rapidly changing world system, pointed out that nothing in a finite world can continue on an exponential curve to infinity. "Civilization is in a transition zone between past exponential growth and some future form of equilibrium."[10] The question is this: When and how will the transition happen? Can we assure some semblance of global stability while the transition completes itself?

1973—Ervin Laszlo, philosopher and systems theorist, warned in *The World System,* "In the remaining decades of this century, mankind's problems will be increasingly complex in detail and global in scope. . . . Never before have so many people faced so many problems of such great complexity. Any attempt to isolate issues and apply short-range remedies will continue to fail by reason of the growing interdependency of all vital processes on this planet."[11] After thus explaining his systems approach to future studies, he asserted: "Concern and controversy over the state of the world is currently growing at an exponential rate. Debate and discussion focuses on the question whether the world system, composed of the human population of the earth together with its technology and life-supporting ecology, can tolerate further growth without limit, or when and how limits to growth must be introduced."[12]

1973—Roberto Vacca, systems mathematician, warned in *The Coming Dark Age,* "It seems very likely, that the most developed nations are on the way toward breakdown on a large scale."[13] He then illustrates dramatic numbers showing the change in global population and also the increasing speed of vehicles. "Similar growth rates are shown by the expanding highway systems, the number of telephones, the number of travelers by air, the number of books printed annually—in short, the numerical membership of any and every class of object and activity.

"All these measurements, then, have the character of continuous and exponential growth, and their variation obeys a well-known mathematical law, the law of the phenomenon of growth in the presence of limiting factors. At first the effect of these limiting factors is hardly noticeable, but there comes a time when they begin to predominate and to produce the phenomenon known as 'saturation'. . . . Often the effect of the limiting factors is not felt gradually: it may be felt all of a sudden."[14] Vacca goes on to say that "ill-equipped planners, unfortunately, work on childishly linear principles when forecasting the future—and then they realize, of course, that the real world has changed much faster than they expected."[15] His prediction is alarmist in tone: "One of my contentions is that the proliferation of large systems until they reach critical, unstable, and uneconomic dimensions will be followed by. . . many catastrophic events."[16]

1976—Herman Kahn, the widely respected heavyweight founder of the Hudson Institute, tried to calm the world and put the whole exponentiality debate to bed in *The Next 200 Years.* "A basic assumption underlying our 400-year earth-centered scenario is that the rates of world population and of economic growth are now close to their historic highs and will soon begin to slow until finally, roughly 100-200 years from now, they will level off in a more or less natural and comfortable way. Such an evolution obviously must have a very different impact upon the prospects for mankind from that of the scenarios currently forecast by many advocates of the limits-to-growth position, who often assume that growth rates will be exponential until limited by physical barriers. . . . There must eventually be limits to population growth which obviously must occur long before such growth would result in a compounding calamity of scarcity, famine, pollution and accompanying social disorder.

"In our view, the resources of the earth will be more than sufficient—with a wide margin of safety—to sustain, for an indefinite period of time and at high living standards, the levels of population and economic growth we project.[17]

"Seen in this perspective, the problem of exponential population growth appears almost to be solving itself."[18] His final conclusion states that "most predictions of damage hundreds of years from now tend to be incorrect because they ignore the curative possibilities inherent in technological and economic progress."[19]

1980—Jeremy Rifkin, a vocal critic of unrestrained technology, picked up the debate in *Entropy*: "The more we try to spread technique over the culture, the more fragmented society becomes. The whole process of increased complexity, increased problems, increased entropy, and increased disorder proceeds exponentially, and that's what makes the modern world crisis so frightening. The exponentiality of the technological fix is a one-way ticket to disaster for life and for the planet earth."[20]

OUR COLLECTIVE YAWN

These obviously were heady days for the cataclysmic crowd. And who could blame them? The math looked ominous.

Then, however, as time went on, the debate began to shift. People began questioning the accuracy of such computer models. First there was skepticism, followed next by derision and sometimes even anger. In response, many limits-to-growth mathematicians quieted down. For despite their warnings, nothing truly catastrophic happened (at least, not on more than a regional scale).

Furthermore, as more evidence poured in we discovered additional important information about how the world system works. This new body of evidence revealed the weaknesses inherent in forecasting and the dangers of over-zealous prognostication. The following list catalogues some of this new evidence.

Complexity—Systems-thinking on a world scale was more complex than first anticipated.

Regionality—The problem of threatened collapse was more a regional threat than global.

Feedback Loops—Negative feedback loops were stronger influences and served as better correctives than first expected.

Equilibrium—Some exponential curves began to level off, transitioning into a new equilibrium. This resulted in what is called an S curve instead of the pure J curve.

Environment—The environment often turned out to be more resilient than we thought. Some environmental problems even began to reverse themselves.

Food—The food supply was dramatically increased on a global scale thanks to the principles of the Green Revolution.

Energy—The anticipated energy shortages never seemed to happen, even despite such occurrences as the OPEC oil embargo in 1973.

Population—As countries developed economically and industrially, their population growth revealed a tendency to level off naturally.

Economy—The world economy showed promise of indefinite expansion.

Reassured that the doomsayers were overly dramatic and not a little premature, we stuffed exponentiality into the back seat. It was headline news in the 1970s, inducing futuristic nightmares. By the 1980s, however, the shock had worn off . . . the sky hadn't fallen. People now began drifting into disinterest, even as the math continued to compound and the curves continued to climb.

By the 1990s, exponentiality made a dramatic economic move, climbing out of the debit column and skillfully relocating itself on the asset side of the ledger. It transitioned from a *bad* topic inducing heartburn and hyperacidity, to a *good* topic inducing an endorphin high. We began to look at exponentiality not as a threat but as a promise. Not as an enemy but as an asset. The entire concept morphed from a depressing topic with apocalyptic implications to an exhilarating topic with prosperous implications.

Now when we heard about exponential growth, we actually *liked* what we heard. Instead of insomnia, we slept well, with dreams of sugar plums and stock markets in our heads. If the population grew exponentially, just imagine what kind of market opportunities that presented! If our bank accounts grew exponentially, what was the matter with that? If global trade and productivity grew by such rapid numbers, no problem! People who discovered how to leverage the exponential curve to their advantage found that, indeed, it took them on a thrilling ride atop a stack of dollar bills rocketing toward the stratosphere.

But perhaps the celebration is premature—I don't think we have heard the end of this story yet. A good piece of advice: Never laugh in the face of a mathematician who is holding a calculator and looking worriedly at the moon.

EXPONENTIALITY, PROFUSION, AND BIG NUMBERS

In our brief historical review of exponentiality, the alarmists focused primarily on several macro-geopolitical issues: population, pollution, energy, resources. Many of their methodologies and conclusions were later challenged and flaws demonstrated. I do not wish to repeat their mistakes and I don't even wish to be identified with their arguments. But they did do us a service by drawing our attention to the fact that *the math is different today*—numbers are bigger, much bigger. And in that sense, Godzilla had it right: size matters.

Now let's take this contemporary New Math—with its massive, wild, unprecedented exponentiality—and apply it to our previous discussion of profusion in chapter 2. To review, profusion is defined as the generalized phenomenon of *more*: more people, more progress, more products, and more of everything else we can think of, all added together. It is important, if we really wish to understand profusion in its cataclysmic fullness, that we open our thinking to include *absolutely everything* that exists in the world system.

Having accumulated everything into one big pile, now let's attempt to somehow measure it all. In fact, as mentioned previously, literally measuring global profusion is impossible—it is too big, it is too inclusive, it changes too rapidly, there are no units to use, and there is no possible mechanism to collect all the data. This of course in no way insinuates that profusion is not a real and objective quantity, but only that it is too profound to measure in any practical sense. Yet, for the important purposes of understanding how profusion changes over time, let's stretch credibility and assume that we succeed in measuring profusion. This measurement, then, we will call the Profusion Number (PN).

In order to arrive at such an inclusive number, we must remember to count all the people, all the progress, all the products, and everything else in the world. For the PN to be accurate, it must include millions of different categories: airbags, golf balls, overhead projectors, credit cards, lawsuits, lost luggage, ice cream cones, food additives, and Websites—to name but a few. Additionally, it must count each individual entry in each category. And this number must be global—each country and each culture must be fully included.

Finally, just when we are confident that nothing has been left out, we will remember a few last entries—key chains, coconuts, every grain of rice eaten by each person in Asia, and every ounce of methane gas produced by cow flatus (which contributes to the atmospheric greenhouse effect). Did you remember to include those things? Once we have added *all* of this together, we have finally computed the PN. This is the number—and nothing less than this number—that I wish to use to measure profusion. I cannot tell you what this number is, but it is greater than a trillion centillion.[21]

EXPONENTIALITY, PROFUSION, AND SPEED

After calculating PN's grand total, next let's look at the issue of speed. Over the years, how rapidly has this number accumulated?

Obviously, this is where exponentiality comes into play.

When we factor in speed, we notice how profusion now must be measured with dimensional numbers usually reserved only for astrophysics. These are the kind of numbers previously reserved to measure phenomenon such as the distance between stars, in units such as light-years.

First, starting at the time of Christ, let's calculate the PN for each of the ensuing 2,000 years. Next, let's graph this number as a function of time. The resultant graph would have a shape approximating the following curve:

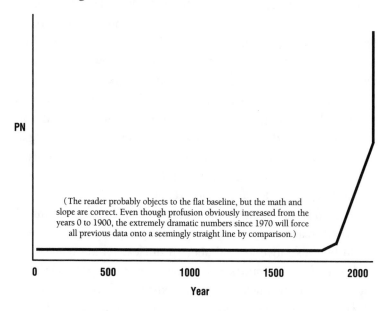

PN

(The reader probably objects to the flat baseline, but the math and slope are correct. Even though profusion obviously increased from the years 0 to 1900, the extremely dramatic numbers since 1970 will force all previous data onto a seemingly straight line by comparison.)

| 0 | 500 | 1000 | 1500 | 2000 |

Year

This graph is dramatic. Actually, I believe it would even be more dramatic than this, a graph slope that is literally a right angle curve. So explosively has the Profusion Number accumulated on our generational shift that it is beyond human capacity for us to grasp it. It is like folding a piece of paper in half one hundred times in five minutes, thus riding a rocket to the far wall of the universe.

REVERSE EXAMPLES

To perhaps help us understand this mathematical phenomenon a bit better, let's engage in what we might call reverse thinking. We usually apply exponential curves to phenomena that grow very fast, thus going from single units to millions and trillions very suddenly.

But let's look at it from a different perspective. Let's apply it to time, and instead of going *up*, let's go *down*. If, for example, something that initially took one hundred years to occur, but was halved with each new occurrence, by the tenth cycle it would take only seventy-one days. By the fortieth cycle, it would take five-thousandths of a second.

When we apply the phenomenon of exponentiality to size dimensions, things get larger very rapidly. But when we apply exponentiality to time dimensions, the durations get shorter very rapidly. Occurrences are now happening virtually overnight.

Understanding this exponentiality of shortening time is essential to understanding my fear for the future. What used to take one hundred years to develop came to take only ten years. Now it takes only ten days—and in some instances ten minutes. And yet because nothing in our routine experience provides us with this type of perspective, we are always surprised.

I stated at the beginning of the chapter that we live in the middle of a chain reaction. Perhaps to more fully appreciate this topic it would be illustrative to read about a nuclear fission reaction. "A nuclear explosion requires an exponentially growing fission chain reaction," explains nuclear weapons expert Richard L. Garwin, "in which a neutron causes fission, producing energy and liberating two or three neutrons, more than one of which on average goes on to cause another fission, and so on. This chain breeding of neutrons and consequent fission is terminated by the disassembly of the system caused by the rapid energy release resulting from the fission process.

"In the fissionable materials used in nuclear weapons, the fission is caused mainly by fast neutrons, which travel only a distance of seven to ten centimeters before colliding with a nucleus, so that each doubling of the neutron population occurs in about 0.01 micro-seconds (one-hundred millionth of a second). The power of compound interest is such that beginning with a single fission, the time required at this doubling interval to cause fission of one kilogram of fissionable material is the time required for eighty such doublings, or less than one microsecond (one millionth of a second). This corresponds to an energy release equivalent to about seventeen kilotons (17,000 tons) of high explosive. The weapon used at Hiroshima produced an energy release equivalent to about fifteen kilotons of high explosive."[22]

In the case described, we have eighty doublings occurring in one-millionth of a second. Think of how explosively destabilizing this is to the plutonium involved. Then realize that this same math is at loose in the world system.

MOVING TARGETS AT THE SPEED OF LIGHT

First, in the early 1970s, we were warned about exponential curves. Then we thought better of the situation and decided to exploit the global markets implicit in such dramatic change. But we have not been careful enough — and we are about to be blind-sided by our own neglect.

Change is not wrong — but not all change is created equal. Exponential change is a class apart. Such a hyperdynamic environment presents us with a perpetually moving target. Our intuition is seldom sufficient — correct that, *never* sufficient — to inform us on issues of this nature. This is why we fail to realize the historically unprecedented changes we are experiencing even though they are happening all around us.

It is my contention that we are living in the middle of an irreversible and exponential "nuclear" explosion with profusion instead of plutonium. In weaponry terms, this is perhaps happening in relative slow motion. But in historic terms, it is happening in the mere blink of an eye.

CHAPTER FIVE

THE FALLENNESS OF THE WORLD SYSTEM

It does not take much in the way of observational powers to realize that the world is a defective place.

Cars break down and people break down. Airplanes crash, computers crash, and stock markets crash. We spray weeds yet they keep coming back. We water plants yet they keep dying. Crops fail from drought or are eaten by bugs. Mother birds sitting on their nests are killed by cats, and the cats are then run over by cars. Tornadoes slash through unsuspecting towns, overturning trailers and killing babies.

Drug dealers become millionaires by knowingly addicting junior-high students. Cigarette executives earn huge paychecks making a product that kills their own friends. Parents abuse their children, who then bring guns to school and kill little girls at point-blank range. The nightly news is nothing more than variations on the same theme: sex and scandals, bullets and body bags, terror and tragedy, wars and rumors of wars.

I assume the vast majority of those reading this book accept the presence of this defect. In theological terms, it is called fallenness (derived from Adam and Eve's "fall" from perfection into sin). British author G. K. Chesterton once said that "the doctrine of the fall is the one Christian belief that is empirically verifiable."[1] Even those not spiritually minded can detect a distortion in the cosmos that consistently thwarts perfection.

THE UTILITY OF UNDERSTANDING FALLENNESS

Because our world is fallen there is at least something wrong with everything. *Nothing* is purely positive. There is a flaw—a defect—inherent in everything on the face of the earth, and the presence of this flaw is universal. It is universal longitudinally across time and it is universal laterally across all human experience.

Albert Einstein once stated that *the law of entropy*, the second law of thermodynamics, is the premier law of all of science. In its own right and in much the same way, we might say that *the law of fallenness* is a premier law in future studies. (It is interesting to reflect on how entropy—a universal principle of decay—and fallenness might be related.)

Without first understanding fallenness, it is impossible to fully understand and explain what is happening in the world around us. It would be like trying to understand infectious disease without first understanding microbes. Previous to the first microscopic sighting of bacteria, everyone understood that if you got a high fever and felt horrible, you might die. But they did not understand *why* this happened. They had not yet isolated the pathogen.

In much the same way, we see that in the world around us, things routinely go wrong. It happens every day to every human in every quadrant of life. Yet until we understand fallenness we don't fully understand *why* this is happening.

Accurately understanding fallenness gives the futurist a tremendous advantage in explaining why things go wrong. As an empiric model, it works. It has the same kind of utility in explaining the course of human history and the current state of the world as gravity has in explaining why objects fall to the earth.

If we wish to understand the dynamics of the world system, fallenness must be factored into our analysis. Furthermore, if we wish to accurately predict the future, fallenness must be carefully integrated into our prognostications. If fallenness is ignored, we place ourselves at significant disadvantage in understanding our current world and our probable future.

FALLENNESS VS. PESSIMISM

It is perhaps worthwhile to differentiate between fallenness and pessimism for they often are confused. When I say there is a defect inherent in *everything*, some would immediately label such a statement as the very definition of pessimism. But there is an important difference between pessimism and fallenness.

Pessimism is a predilection to take the darkest view of things, to choose the gloomiest of all options, to always see the negative rather than the positive, to accept whatever interpretation is the most onerous, to believe that evil outweighs good.

Fallenness, on the other hand, simply acknowledges that things are inherently defective. It does not say that this defect always prevails (as pessimism often does). It doesn't refuse to acknowledge the beauty and happiness in the world (as pessimism often does).

Pessimism maintains that the good *will not* win; fallenness maintains that the good *might not* win. Pessimism maintains that nothing is ultimately promising; fallenness maintains that nothing is ultimately pure.

Some people are markedly phobic about pessimism, taking great pains to avoid any hint of it in their language, attitude, or philosophy. But in their strenuous attempts to distance themselves from pessimism, they occasionally end up also denying the existence of fallenness. For us to package pessimism with fallenness and then throw them both out together is a serious error, especially if we want credibility as futurists.

Another common reaction against pessimism is to swing to the opposite extreme by endorsing total optimism. But if pessimism often *over*-acknowledges the reality of fallenness, optimism often *under*-acknowledges it. Neither pole serves the futurist well.

Pessimists are hampered in their assessments because they cannot realistically acknowledge the goodness and beauty of the world. Optimists are likewise hampered in their assessments because they cannot realistically acknowledge the baseness and evil in the world.

The reader needs to know that I regard myself as neither a pessimist nor an optimist. My studied intention is to be a realist. I strive *to see things as they are*—not as I *fear* them to be (the pessimist approach) and not as I *wish* them to be (the optimist approach).

The realism I am after is the realism related to accuracy. Such accuracy is as essential in future studies as it is in medicine. Let me give you an illustration. If a patient comes into my office with weight loss and abdominal pain, to arrive at a truthful diagnosis I need to find out the actual pathology behind the symptoms. Just because many patients dread cancer does not mean that I should attempt to accommodate their fears by not considering malignancy. To not think seriously about cancer with such symptoms is foolish and perhaps even malpractice.

But, on the other hand, cancer is not the only diagnosis that should come to my mind. There are many possible benign etiologies that might be causing these symptoms. And even if biopsies indeed turn out to be cancerous, such a diagnosis is not automatically a death sentence. Many cancers are curable.

So, as we often see in medicine, a patient might come in *fearing* the worst (the pessimistic approach) or *ignoring* the worst (the optimistic approach). My job is to turn a deaf ear toward their bias and discover what *is*. In this sense, pessimism and optimism have nothing to contribute in the assessment and indeed only get in the way of diagnostic accuracy.

Just because we acknowledge pain and problems does not mean that we are being pessimistic. It is better called realism. For example, it is not pessimism to say that if we jumped from an airplane without a parachute we would die—it is realism. It is not pessimism to say that if we try to swim the Pacific Ocean we would drown—it is pure logic. It is not pessimism to say that if our church built a hundred-million-dollar gymnasium we would go bankrupt—it is truth. It is not pessimism to say that the future will manifest fallenness—it is an easily established fact.

Fallenness is the only way to adequately explain the widespread defect that manifests itself at every turn in the affairs of humankind. We have never had a stretch of human history that did not offer abundant evidence for fallenness. Similarly, *there never will be a stretch of human future without fallenness manifesting itself.*

FALLENNESS AND OUR FUTURE

When we understand fallenness, then we understand why things so often end up flawed in mysterious ways. We understand why the many advantages we have in progress still do not completely offset the serious problems in the world system. We understand why, with each new "thing" profusion adds to the world stage, there is a downside that must be acknowledged, anticipated, and dealt with. We understand why Utopia did not show up as expected.

Again, the idea of fallenness contends that nothing is one hundred percent pure or innocent. All things—whether toothpicks or telephones, antibiotics or automobiles—must be associated with either an *actualized* fallenness or at least a *potential* fallenness.

Consider the humble toothpick. Toothpicks are small and unassuming, seemingly quite innocent. They are used daily by millions, if not billions. But even the toothpick has a fallenness defect. They can, for example, cause gum disease. They can seed the blood stream with bacteria leading to heart damage. When swallowed, they can cause bowel obstruction, perforation, peritonitis, and death. The toothpick, it turns out, is mostly innocent—but not pure. It lives in a fallen world and has taken on that defect.

How about telephones? They facilitate relationships and deepen community. They connect the lonely and rescue the critically ill. But drug lords also use them to conduct business. Crime bosses continue their work from prison cells via contraband cell phones. Prostitution services have been run by cell phone from college class. Teenagers have amassed huge bills by calling 1-900 phone sex lines. Dinner interruptions, wrong numbers, unwanted telemarketers, noise pollution—telephones, too, exist in a fallen world.

Antibiotics, of course, have saved millions of lives. Who could argue with antibiotics? But when we apply the principle of fallenness to penicillin, for example, we see that it too has an associated fallenness defect. Every year, penicillin kills people from allergic reactions. Penicillin can cause drug resistant bacteria to emerge. In addition, it can result in "nausea, vomiting, epigastric distress, diarrhea, black hairy tongue, skin eruptions, urticaria, fever, hemolytic anemia, leukopenia, nephropathy, thrombocytopenia, and anaphylaxis." You could, along with the *Physicians' Desk Reference*, call these "Adverse Reactions." But you could just as accurately call them manifestations of fallenness.

Automobiles are functional, fast, and fun. We can't even begin to imagine modern life without their services. But flat tires in snowstorms are not fun. Nor are overheated radiators, exploding batteries, bent valves, or thrown rods. Infants left inside cars in parking lots on hot days have suffocated to death. Airbags have decapitated babies. Some people reading this sentence will not live out the year, ushered into the next world by a car out of control. Automobiles are not free from the fallenness defect.

The world is a defective, fallen place. Things go wrong. It happens all the time.

NATURAL EVIL AND MORAL EVIL

Much of what goes wrong in life is clearly traceable to human acts of wrongdoing. This is called *moral evil*, and as such it is intentional and therefore avoidable.

At other times, however, the etiology of our problems seems amorphous. Many of our difficulties do not result from human malice or corruption. In these instances, fallenness just shows up unexpectedly, making a sudden appearance in the routine course of events. These accidental and unanticipated negative consequences are called *natural evil*.

Let's briefly examine these two categories, as each will help us better understand the potential future problems inherent in the fallenness defect.

Natural Evil

Many of the daily problems that confound our existence and frustrate our daily affairs cannot be blamed on human misconduct. They are not intentional and they come uninvited. These complications of fallenness are often labeled *natural evil*—adverse happenings that are accidental, unanticipated, and unavoidable. NASA officials, for example, did not want the space shuttle Challenger to explode. No one set out to knock a hole in our ozone or intentionally pollute our rivers. Most of the problems illustrated with toothpicks, telephones, antibiotics, and automobiles would also be included in this subset of fallenness.

The general and often frightening rule of *unanticipated consequences* fits prominently into this category, as explained in my earlier book *Margin*: "We cannot foresee the unforeseen. We did not know acid rain would result from burning fossil fuels. We did not know PCBs in fish would not be metabolized away. We did not know mobility would disrupt family and community stability. We did not know inner city housing projects would turn into ghetto war zones. We did not know thalidomide would deform babies. We did not invent suburbs to throw our traffic patterns into chaos."[2]

The future will always hold surprises. Many of our problems are simply that—surprises. Many of our current afflictions—on both a national and global level—can be traced back to good intentions and what might be called "positive origins." Because of fallenness and natural evil, however, even our best intentions often backfire.

Alarmingly, even the *solutions* to our problems often have unanticipated consequences of their own. "Our solutions intensify the problems they were intended to solve or create new and more serious problems," remarks economist Bob Goudzwaard.[3] In this way, history sometimes unfolds counterintuitively. We once thought science would solve all our problems. It has indeed solved many but created additional ones, from weaponry to pollution. Antibiotics have resulted in widespread microbial resistance. Abundant inexpensive food has resulted in unprecedented obesity. Important legislative protections have resulted in legal complexity and paralysis. Needed social service programs have led to bureaucracies and welfare dependency. Health care improvements have resulted in staggering health care costs.

No conspiracy is responsible for putting E. coli O157 in our meat or inducing skin cancer from the sun's rays. Such things just come from living in a fallen world.

Moral Evil

As we have seen, many of our pains emerge from accidental, natural causes. This, however, in no way diminishes the culpability of humankind, for our most bitter pains arise from our own moral failures. Despite the best efforts of progress, these *moral evils*—intentional and avoidable—still abound. Education, affluence, and technology have not diminished their deadly powers.

We do not give our five-year-olds real guns to play with. They are not wise, and someone might get hurt. Yet progress has put weapons in the hands of our fallenness, giving us incredible power without regard to wisdom. Unfortunately, power and maturity are not linked. Ten years more modernization brings untold increases in power but no guaranteed improvement in virtue. This has not been a stabilizing development.

As a direct result of these "weapons," evil today has more power than ever before. One thousand years ago, Saddam Hussein could only have carried a spear; today, he can wreak widespread destruction with the nod of his head. It is only one man, but evil is more powerful.

The malicious use of such increased power is seen globally in every country, and it is found on many fronts: economics, politics, entertainment, research, the military. We see it in drug kingpins, giant industrial polluters, rock music idols, and Hollywood movie producers. Their strength and powerbase come largely from affluence, technology, and the media. "All our knowledge has not ushered in a brave new world," maintains Prison Fellowship founder, Charles Colson. "It has simply increased our ability to perpetrate evil."[4]

That the good and bad often travel together is vexatious and frustrating in the extreme. Yet reality demonstrates this is always the case. In his essay *Is Progress Possible?* British scholar C. S. Lewis concluded: "We shall grow able to cure, and to produce, more diseases — bacterial war, not bombs, might ring down the curtain — to alleviate, and to inflict, more pains, to husband, or to waste, the resources of the planet more extensively. We can become either more beneficent or more mischievous. My guess is we shall do both; mending one thing and marring another, removing old miseries and producing new ones, safeguarding ourselves here and endangering ourselves there."[5]

DEEPENING THE DILEMMA

So far we have noticed that:

- Fallenness is ubiquitous — it is everywhere.
- As a concept, fallenness has great utility in helping us understand why things go wrong.

- Fallenness has both a natural evil component and a moral
  evil component.

In addition, there are several other implications of fallenness that
might be considered for the purposes of understanding our com-
plicated and ominous future.

The Failure of Progress to Remove Fallenness

Progress has put on a spectacular economic-educational-techno-
logical show over the past two centuries and we are all beneficiaries.
I am not demeaning this performance, for the record of achieve-
ment has been truly impressive. But eliminating fallenness has not
been among progress's accomplishments.

The entire chronicle of the human race has been marked by selfishness, treachery, and bloodshed. There has never been an era
where this has not been true. But the twentieth century has witnessed more spectacular selfishness, treachery, and bloodshed than
any other time in history, leaving many moderns disillusioned and
cynical. If progress has put on a show, fallenness has put on quite
a spectacular show of its own.

I see no reason either historically or theologically to believe
that God will suspend the law of fallenness as a concession to
progress. The only possible reason why God would honor progress
with such an exemption would be if progress were honoring Him.
And such is not the case.

The Fallacy of Problem Diminution

No matter how many problems we solve, we never run out of them.
For example, when one problem is solved in quadrant A, a second
problem breaks out in quadrant B. We solve problem 5, then problem 50, then problem 500. But no matter how many problems we
solve, we never run out of problems.

In my clinical medical work, for example, I have solved

patient problems on a daily basis for twenty years. Yet patients generate new problems as fast as I solve the old ones.

Likewise, in my academic medical work I solved problems on a daily basis for fifteen years—and I am a good problem solver. Nevertheless, I never came to work and found that the residency had been so perfected that there was nothing left to do. No matter how many problems I solved the day before, my problem list never went away. And no matter how many problems I had solved, the medical residents were just as unhappy as ever.

My patients, the clinic, and the residents are not being malicious here. It is simply that we all live in a broken world, and no amount of human effort can fix the break. Fallenness just keeps coming back for more.

The Expanding Power of Evil

When the concept of exponentiality is applied to money, speed, technology, and power, progress is clearly benefited. But evil flourishes as well. Any serious futurist must take into account the following discomforting linkage:

Humankind is flawed and capable of limitless acts of evil,

and

Progress exponentially increases the power available for the purposes of evil.

If we could graph the expanding power that evil has available at its disposal, what might that graph look like? It is the stuff nightmares are made of. Consider this: From 1500 to the present, the amount of potential power accessible at a single explosive detonation—a single "*boom*"—has increased ten billion times. This power is accessible for the purposes of good, but is equally accessible for the purposes of evil.

THE DESTABILIZATION OF OUR FUTURE

Progress always and irreversibly gives us more and more of everything faster and faster. This includes more power, more technology, and more money. In addition, the world always has more people. All of this is happening exponentially.

Some of these people will be thoroughly and unrepentantly evil. And these thoroughly evil people will use this exponentially increasing power, technology, and money to advance their evil purposes. Faster and faster.

Over the past two hundred years, progress has been both helping us out and lifting us up. But lurking in the shadows of progress, fallenness has been swallowing steroids and pumping iron. It has not been a stabilizing development.

We are not finished building our case for the end of the age, however. Instead, the fallenness plank is but one more trestle laid on the bridge under construction. So take another swallow of antacid and read on.

CHAPTER SIX

A PROFUSION OF NEGATIVE

We have already examined the concept of profusion, defined as the generalized phenomenon of *more*: more people, more progress, more products, and more of everything else you can think of, all added together. We have seen that if this profusion were graphed over time, it would be an exponential curve in the extreme, increasing (if I may borrow a scientific concept for effect) at the speed of light. The increase would be so dramatic that nothing in previous human experience could equal it, thus leaving us seriously behind the curve in understanding it and leaving us consistently below reality in underestimating it.

In addition, we have examined how everything in a fallen world is itself fallen. This does not imply that some things are not *good*—but simply that nothing is *purely good*. Even things that are considered "good" are fallen, and they manifest this fallenness often. Modern jetliners crash. Honest citizens go bankrupt. Virtuous church leaders get cancer. Heroes get caught in scandals. Outstanding families are killed in automobile accidents. In a fallen world, all things are tainted. All things are defective, flawed, . . . fallen.

As the next step in constructing a proof for the end of the age, let's combine the two principles above: that profusion is continuously giving us more of everything increasing exponentially, and that each component entity of profusion is fallen. When we combine the two, we now notice that the total amount of fallenness (either actualized or potential) is increasing rapidly along with the profusion.

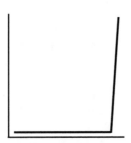

Total Fallenness vs. Time

With this ever-increasing profusion in the world system, we also have a profusion of the negative in each of these new things. Again — and I must emphasize this so you do not misunderstand me — this is *not* to say that there isn't much good in all that profusion is bringing us. People, progress, and products can be beneficial and delightful. However, it is my strong assertion that with each new entity there is both good and bad, positive and negative, blessing and curse mixed together. Thus while progress brings ever-increasing positive, it also brings *ever-increasing negative*. And this, in many cases, is happening with frightening suddenness.

What are the implications of such dramatically increasing profusion when we factor in fallenness? It is a legitimate and daunting question.

THE INCREASING EXPRESSION OF FALLENNESS

Some people believe in the notion that because we are "modern," fallenness must be receding. But it is not possible to overcome fallenness with modernity, and it is not possible to overcome fallenness with profusion. Let me attempt to illustrate this mathematically. If we have *one million* people with *x units* of progress, what would happen to fallenness if we increased this to *one billion* people with x^2 *units* of progress? Will fallenness fade and then disappear as we have more people with more progress? This is, at face value, a ridiculous notion. Yet it is precisely what many have been hoping for and assuming will happen.

As another example, if we have one hundred cars in a town (call it Centerville, USA) and we wanted to *decrease* the chances that they would crash, would *increasing* the number of cars to one thousand help accomplish this goal? If there were one hundred movies shown throughout the year in Centerville cinemas and we wanted to *decrease* the total amount of violence and nudity presented throughout the year, would *increasing* the number of movies to one thousand help accomplish such a decrease? Obviously not.

Profusion inevitably leads to an increasing opportunity for fallenness to express itself. This does not mean that fallenness necessarily *will* increasingly express itself—but the opportunity clearly exists.

GRAVITY AND FALLENNESS

Let me attempt to make the same point through a different illustration. Suppose we were to take a single baseball high above the earth's surface and drop it. What would happen? Obviously, it would fall to earth.

Now, suppose that for some reason we wanted to decrease the gravitational pull on the ball. How might we accomplish such a goal? If we increased the number of baseballs to one hundred, hoping that somehow by *increasing* the number of balls we would be *decreasing* the pull of gravity on each ball, would that work? Obviously not. If we had one ball, one hundred balls, or one million balls—all would fall at the same rate, influenced by the same pull.

In this sense, gravity and fallenness are similar (no pun intended). Gravity exerts the same pull on each object regardless of the number of objects brought into its pull. Gravity itself is not diminished but instead we see an increase in the number of objects brought under its influence. Fallenness, likewise, is not lessened by increasing the number of objects. Instead, we simply have more objects being influenced by fallenness.

In fact, *each object that profusion introduces into the world's system is equally affected by fallenness.* I am not saying that the manifestation of fallenness would be identical—obviously there is a difference in potential mischief between a fallen toothpick and a fallen nuclear weapon. But I am saying that in the same way that gravity exerts a consistent and measurable pull on all objects coming into its field, so every object existing in a fallen world finds itself affected by the "pull" of that fallenness.

MORE PEOPLE, MORE FALLENNESS

One result of profusion is that there are more people. This is a powerful, irreversible trend manifested in the world system since the beginning of history. And it is *not evil!* I am not objecting to this trend. We were told by God to populate the earth. So we have.

At the time of Christ, the world's population was about 140 million people. By the year 1000 A.D., the population had doubled. At the turn of the millennium, we now have more than six billion people.

Each of these people is a separate, individual moral agent. Each is capable of good, noble, virtuous behavior, just as each is capable of reflecting fallenness. Will increasing the total number of people on the earth automatically result in decreasing fallenness? Even for the fallenness problem to hold at its present level, it would require that the amount of fallenness in each person lessen somewhat with each new birth. And that, obviously, does not happen. With more people, for example, there are more crimes. (In the United States, fifty years ago we had less than 200,000 prisoners; today we have 1.7 million.) With more people there are more bankruptcies. (Fifty years ago we had 20,000 bankruptcies annually; today we have 1.3 million.)[1] There are more car accidents, and more people killed in those accidents. There are more people killed by disease.

Most shockingly, in this century there have been between 120 million and 200 million "man-made" deaths from acts of war, terrorism, and governments killing their own people. This figure far exceeds any such numbers from previous centuries. Fallenness coupled with profusion (more people, more technology, more weapons, more mobility, more speed, and so on) has allowed savagery at a level impossible for previous centuries.

TAKING THE BAD WITH THE GOOD

Everything in life can be submitted to a positive/negative analysis. In a fallen world both come together, whether we like it or not. When we grow wheat there will also be weeds. Let's briefly study four representative examples to further demonstrate how this works in real life.

Technology

Positive: The average American must learn how to operate 20,000 pieces of technology in his or her lifetime. Many of these are wonderfully entertaining. Others, laborsaving, timesaving, or productivity enhancing.

Negative: The manifestations of fallenness involved in technology are legion—broken components, noise, cost, complexity, dehumanization. Many devices were seemingly "designed to infuriate." Information technology has contributed to accessibility overload, with the average worker today receiving 169 messages a day—enough to drive us to the brink.

Internet

Positive: The information superhighway will solve many problems with education, communication, research, marketing, even international commerce. Beyond information dissemination and E-mail, people can now book their own airline tickets, shop on-line, and even develop their own cyber-communities.

Negative: E-mail overload is becoming a serious problem, with some busy users reporting 250 messages a day. Spamming, or junk E-mail, is maddening. Shopping on-line risks security breeches for credit card accounts. Internet addiction keeps people from investing in real life. Hate groups use the Internet to propagandize. Hackers have penetrated corporate computers as well as computers of government agencies, including the Pentagon. Pornography is viciously accessible via the Internet with one adult entertainment website reporting an estimated 1.4 *billion* hits last year.

Mobility

Positive: Most people appreciate the ability to get in a car and visit a friend in the next county, or to jump on a plane and explore a canyon six states away. Mobility allows us to change jobs when needed, to escape geography and climate when needed, or to start over when needed.

Negative: Mobility has had a devastating effect on community, on rootedness, on tradition, on job longevity, and on church relationships. Mobility has allowed kidnappers and pedophiles to roam thousands of miles in search of their next victims. Mobility has contributed to the spread of disease, including virulent strains of influenza and HIV. Almost all microbes have incubation periods long enough to permit international travel anywhere in the world before clinical symptoms begin, thus greatly increasing the risk of global pandemics.

Longevity

Positive: Our increasing life expectancy for the United States—and more recently the entire world—has been dramatic. (0 A.D.–21 years; 1900–47 years; 2000–76 years).[2] The elderly are healthier and wealthier than ever before, and their presence among us is a blessing for our entire society.

Negative: Dramatically increased life expectancy also results in a serious and rapidly increasing problem financing Social Security and Medicare. Also, because our "halfway" technologies can keep us from dying but not completely cure our disease, tens of millions now live with chronic diseases. Many of our aged wish God would call them home.

No matter what topic we choose, it is possible to go through the same process and find the good and the bad growing side by side. Some people might object to this type of critical analysis: "What kind of ingratitude is this? This is morbid pessimism!" I certainly don't want to be accused of neglecting the benefits that have accrued as a result of progress. These benefits are real and should not be dismissed. But I will draw us back once more to the thesis of the book—we are exploring the end of the age, not the glories of progress. If the world is being propelled toward a cataclysmic end, it is best that we stay on task.

I am not intending to be unbalanced against the good, but instead to take a long, hard, objective, measured look at the flaws in life and to then project where they might be leading us. There can be no dispute that the incredible numbers which profusion is generating will lead to massive growth opportunities for fallenness. If fallenness were a stock, this might be a good time to buy.

WHAT CAN BLUNT FALLENNESS?

So, to be perfectly clear about it, I am not saying that progress has been useless or futile. I am not saying that progress and its resultant profusion are not God's will for human activity. I am not saying that development, differentiation, and proliferation are not normative human activities, even spiritually speaking. I am not saying that we should stop having children. I am not saying that populating the earth is an evil thing to do. I am not saying that we should stop healing disease, discovering antibiotics, building roads, and inventing machines.

What I am saying is this: as we continue with progress and profusion; as we continue with development, differentiation, and proliferation; as we continue populating the earth by having children; as we continue healing disease, discovering antibiotics, building roads, and inventing machines, let us soberly realize that fallenness is maddeningly persistent. Let us realize that so very often in a fallen world, as we alleviate problems in one area, we simultaneously compound problems in another area. Let us realize that as we have our children, none of us is pure and surely none of them will be pure. They will, Lord willing, contribute to godliness—but they will also invariably contribute to fallenness.

What can deliver us then? Can progress? No. Can global economic growth and health care? No. Can universal education and social learning? No. Can international negotiations? No. Each of these things has something to contribute in addressing the problems of humanity. Progress, for example, can indeed make life better in thousands of ways. Economic growth and health care can alleviate much suffering. Education and social learning have proven value. International negotiations have kept us out of a world war for more than fifty years—an impressive record.

But none of these things can negate the pervasive and malignant effects of fallenness. Even as they make life better, they simultaneously give fallenness thousands of new, faster, more powerful ways to express itself. None of these things can or ever will defeat fallenness. Only a power that transcends this fallen reality—only God Himself—can do that.

Life under the tutelage of progress is getting better: The positive is growing at a rapid rate. But, at precisely the same time, fall-enness is becoming more powerful: The negative is also growing at a rapid rate.

If we re-examine two earlier graphs—the profusion number (page 65) and total fallenness vs. time (page 82)—we notice that both are growing exponentially. This is easily provable mathematically. But what about isolating and then graphing the component of good we find in profusion? Such a graph would reveal that the good too is growing rapidly, even exponentially.

It is natural to hope that the good is growing faster than the bad—and indeed I think it is. It is also completely natural to hope that the good will continue to grow faster than the bad—and again, I think it will.

But that does not mean we are safe.

CHAPTER SEVEN

THE THRESHOLD OF LETHALITY

Every person, no matter how optimistically inclined, would have to yield in debate that, yes, in fact things do consistently go wrong in the world. Even if we don't wish to call it fallenness, or even if we militantly believe and defend optimism, nevertheless we would still have to admit that bad things happen. If we prefer to avoid the word fallenness, we might call it The Flaw—defined as that philosophical presence (actualized or potential) that exists in each thing which, when manifested, results in problems, suffering, disease, evil, or death.

Granting the presence of such fallenness, if we wish to defend progress and all its benefits against my thesis as presented so far, perhaps the best rhetorical approach would be the following:

- Yes, fallenness is real and maddeningly ubiquitous.
- With progress, however, the good outweighs and outnumbers the bad.

This is the most plausible forensic approach that I can think of.

It is, in fact, the tack I would take if attempting to defend progress and its role in our future. I would take such an approach because it is largely true—the good outweighs and outnumbers the bad.

Most people are good people. They do, by far, more good than bad. Most medical discoveries bring more good than bad. Most antibiotics have far greater therapeutic benefits than adverse reactions. Most new technologies are more beneficial than "infuriating." Most cars are good cars. Most trips taken with these good cars are successful and uneventful. Sure, flat tires and overheated engines happen, and the world will never be one hundred percent free of these irritations. But such events are rare enough that our continued use of automobiles is clearly justified.

Yes, with increasing profusion perhaps the overall amount of *fallenness* associated with that profusion mathematically increases. But the *good* of profusion (and progress) mathematically increases faster—far faster. This is, in fact, the very definition of progress. Not perfection, but betterment. Consistent, continuous betterment. The good growing faster than the bad.

THE SEPARATE ACCOUNTING OF GOOD AND BAD

Most people automatically think that if the good outweighs and outnumbers the bad, we are better off. For example, if a new entity (discovery, product, trend, and so forth) brings one hundred units of gain and only ten units of harm, then we have a net positive. Therefore we should welcome such an entity into our world.

But herein lies a trap, one that has escaped the attention of most futurists. The path of reasoning must be carefully chosen lest we stumble into this trap on our way to a conclusion. The trap has to do with the accounting method commonly used to calculate positives versus negatives.

If we were to use standard accounting methods in analyzing this labyrinthine snarl called modernity, we would add up all the credits and subtract the debits. When the resultant balance is positive, we say that a gain has been realized. This accounting method, however, is not always accurate. When applied to contemporary conditions this method can be dangerously misleading.

If we listed all the positives of progress, it would be a very long list. There can be no question that we enjoy many advantages over previous generations. The trouble is revealed, however, when we begin to tabulate the negatives. Here we find such a daunting list of problems that they threaten the viability of our entire society.

In light of this, I wish to proprose the following axiom for your consideration:

> If the negatives are sufficiently dangerous, they cannot be offset by the positives *no matter how beneficial the positives are.*

We cannot simply subtract the negatives from the positives and look at the sum. The negatives *must* be accounted on their own.

To further illustrate this principle in a more visible manner, let's assume that we somehow are able to accumulate all the positives into one pile and all the negatives into an adjacent pile. Now let's step back and examine the two piles. Our usual habit is to say that if the pile of positive is bigger than the pile of negative we have "progressed." Such is not always the case.

In some instances, yes, this simplistic analysis yields an accurate conclusion. But in other important instances, this reasoning is dangerously flawed. It is in this second instance that *we must look at the pile of negative completely independent of the pile of positive.* If we fail to grasp this principle, we will also fail to anticipate the cataclysmic dangers of our future.

For example, Ralph is a bank president with a seven-figure salary, a swimming pool, clean coronary arteries, a stable marriage, good kids, a post-graduate degree, and a daily limousine. But one night a thief comes into his house and kills him. No matter how much "benefit" Ralph had piled up, the "detriment" still won. Death has a way of trumping progress.

SCENARIOS TO CONSIDER

To better understand this axiom, let's examine additional scenarios which illustrate the point in everyday terms.

Scenario: Great Fishing

Being a lover of fishing, you form a group of volunteer sportsmen who set about to improve the fish habitat in your area lake. First you sink fish cribs that allow small fish to feed while escaping predators. Next, you start a fish hatchery. When hatchlings grow to optimal size you release them into the lake. Next you protect the natural spawning beds. You clean all the carp out of the lake. You optimize the food source. You modify aquatic vegetation to benefit the fish. You shut down the polluting factory upriver that has been dumping unregulated chemicals for years. You institute minimum size limits for keeping fish caught. Finally, you encourage catch-and-release.

There is only one problem. A gasoline tank truck driving over the bridge blows a tire, careens over the wall, and falls into the lake. All the gasoline escapes into the water. Fish kill: 100 percent.

Comment: Ten systematic improvements versus only one random, spontaneous negative. Yet the negative won.

Scenario: Great Mailbox

You go to the mailbox and find ten letters addressed with your name. The first announces that you just inherited one million dollars. A second informs you that your book proposal was accepted by the publisher. A third letter sends the delightful news that your oldest child was just accepted into a top university with full scholarship. Each letter in turn brings good news: Your godchild became engaged, your lost pet was found, your new BMW finally arrived at the dealership.

There is only one problem. Your last letter—from the Public Health Department—contains the results of your HIV test: positive, from an inadvertent needle stick.

Comment: The positive letter to negative letter ratio was 9:1. Does that mean that you are better off?

Scenario: Great Vacation

You sell your home, quit your job, and fly to the Caribbean. After five years of planning, your spouse and teenage children are thrilled at the prospect of island hopping on a fifty-foot sailboat for the next twelve months. This is not a lark: Together you took sailing, navigation, and scuba lessons and have even read books about the islands. You have studied Caribbean cuisine and learned a bit of Patois.

There is only one problem. During a short rainstorm with mildly gusty seas, you are blown slightly off course, hit a reef, and tear a hole in the bottom of the boat. The boat sinks in sixty seconds, and your youngest child drowns.

Comment: It was only one short storm for only one short hour with only one small unmarked reef. Everything else was perfect. Does the good outweigh the bad?

You finally finish your dream house after ten years and ten million dollars—but a lightning strike burns it to the ground in ten minutes. You train for the Olympic marathon while putting your life, your family, and your career on hold—but a stress fracture the week before your event forces you out of competition. You have a prestigious job at Harvard University, making stunning discoveries in astrophysics and being mentioned for a Nobel Prize—but your teenage son commits suicide.

If you will concede my point, I will stop depressing you with these morbid illustrations. If you will not yet concede, however, realize that the number of illustrations is almost infinite and I can go on for a very long time.

No matter how large the quantity or quality of positive, if the negative is harmful enough, it wins. If the negative reaches a level severe enough, then it has the power to disqualify the entire experience. It is instructive to realize that *increasing the positive will usually not lessen the disqualifying character of the negative.* It must, therefore, be regarded separately when doing assessments.

Clarifying this principle also sheds light on a related but often mysterious societal phenomenon. Why do some people seem to "have it all" and then quit? Often it is because the advantage (money, fame, prestige) doesn't any longer offset the damage (stress, frustration, overload, long hours, lack of privacy, hostile press, alienation from the family). Professional sports heroes, movie stars, politicians, corporate executives—there is a point where the amount of positive is no longer the determining factor. It is the extent of negative. And the negative cannot be offset by simply increasing the positive. The "bad" will still be disqualifying no matter how much "good" is added on.

THRESHOLD OF LETHALITY

As we have seen, the negative must be accounted separately because under certain conditions, it wins. But we must carry this discussion at least one step further, for not all negative is created equal: Some is merely noxious; some is morbid; and some is lethal. It is this latter category which we must now concern ourselves with.

The positives of progress bring blessing, but the negatives bring pain. And once these negatives reach a certain critical mass, they bring death. This level is what I call the *threshold of lethality.* And nothing can offset lethality once it has occurred.

A fifty-year-old man from Albuquerque might have a marvelous body, perfectly functioning in all respects. He cares for it by regular exercise and eight hours of sleep per night. He is fastidious about his diet: no donuts, no Twinkies, no potato chips. He has great blood pressure, has low cholesterol, and takes antioxidants. He gets regular EKGs, has memorized all the American

Cancer Society guidelines, and is up-to-date on all his immunizations. He gets regular physical exams. Even his doctor hints that he is perhaps being too careful.

One day, however, he comes down with a fever. He has a mild sore throat, aching muscles, and a headache. Then he starts to cough. By the time he goes to the clinic, he is short of breath. A chest x-ray reveals massive bilateral infiltrates. He is admitted to the ICU where despite intensive therapy, his blood oxygen drops—and he dies. Culture and blood work later reveal a virulent respiratory virus, picked up while wilderness camping.

This man followed every health rule in the book. But in the end it did not matter. All the positive of his healthy habits did not matter once the negative reached a level of lethality. Beyond the health and fitness regimens he observed, he also had a Harvard MBA degree on the wall, a Range Rover in the garage, and a generous 401(k) plan in his back pocket. They didn't help much either. In the end, the lethality of the virus overwhelmed everything.

MACROBAD AND MEGASUICIDE

The illustrations above all involve small scale experiences. We might call them local events or mini-illustrations. But the principle of lethality also applies to much larger systems: nations, economies, political parties, entire biological species. Billion-dollar companies go bankrupt overnight. Ethnic populations suffer genocide. Large segments of oceans become sterile. Species extinction happens regularly.

Let's take it one step further. Beyond the regional and national, what about on the global level? Is there such a thing as a threshold of lethality for the entire world system? Of course. A large asteroid, for example, could raise enough atmospheric debris to cause a "nuclear winter" effect and global extinction.

Asteroidal collisions are examples of "natural disasters" that could bring global extinction. Such natural disasters, however, are not the focus of this book, for statistically they have nothing to do with progress, profusion, exponentiality, or fallenness (except as included under the "natural evil" category).

Instead we are concerned with man-made and human-influenced disasters capable of causing cataclysmic destruction. Several scenarios present themselves for immediate consideration: war (especially involving nuclear, biological, and chemical weapons, the so-called *weapons of mass destruction*), disease, and environmental catastrophes. These are perhaps the most likely players in any global lethality scenario, and they will be explored in more detail later.

FALLENNESS WITH A GUN

No matter how many benefits of progress the world system enjoys, and no matter how rapidly these benefits accumulate, once the negatives rise to the level of lethality the viability of the entire globe will be threatened. Lethality is not intimidated by progress. Perhaps that's not fair, but lethality is like that.

Progress has put on a dramatic show and produced spectacular benefits. In the race to the future, surely progress has a commanding lead. But there is one problem. Someone gave fallenness a gun. And we all know that fallenness has the will to shoot progress in the back.

CHAPTER EIGHT

THEREFORE . . .

In each chapter to this point, my primary objective has been fairly narrow—namely to convince the reader of the thesis of that particular chapter. It has been my intent for you to understand the independent validity of profusion, then of irreversibility, then of exponentiality, and so forth on stand-alone grounds. But this has been only step one of a two-step process: first, to build a compelling case for the validity of each individual component of the argument, and second, to demonstrate the necessary and inevitable linkage between these components. We have now arrived at this second step.

If you have been reading with sufficient carryover from one chapter to the next, it is perhaps already clear how I intend to link these components together thus constructing my argument for the end of the age. But for the sake of completeness, let's review the various steps and construct that proof now. It is not really a complex argument, but that does not mean it is easy to grasp the flow of the argument as an integrated whole.

Profusion—The world is always, and unavoidably, experiencing an ever-increasing profusion. There are more people, more products, more technology, more information, more air miles traveled, more toothpicks—more of everything. Although many forces contribute to the phenomenon, profusion is largely due to progress—working through the twin engines of differentiation and proliferation—giving us more and more of everything faster and faster.

Both progress and profusion are generally considered to be positive developments in the advancement of the human race—a sentiment with which I do not disagree.

Irreversibility—The trend toward ever-increasing profusion, toward *more*, is irreversible. If we were to objectively measure global profusion over the past one hundred years we would notice a steady, relentless, inexorable increase. There has never been a factor in the historical experience of the last century that has been able to stop the advance of profusion. And those factors that have slowed profusion—for example, economic downturns, infectious epidemics, or oppressive governments—have usually been regional rather than global, and have always been temporary rather than permanent.

Not only has the historical course of profusion been irreversible, but it also has been consistently accelerating—all in the upward direction.

Exponentiality—If we were able to graph profusion we would see that the resulting curve is exponential in the extreme. The growth of profusion currently is increasing so dramatically that there is no other measurable commodity in human experience that can approximate such a growth rate. This leaves us with an unprecedented phenomenon unlike any the world system has ever before experienced.

Exponential curves, in general, are difficult for us to anticipate. They are thus almost always underestimated. And yet the exponentiality of profusion (that is, Profusion Number) exceeds that of most other exponential curves by several orders of magnitude. It is humanly impossible for us to even begin to imagine exponentiality on this level. The growth of this curve is rising so rapidly we might use as a mental image something between a rocket blast and the speed of light.

Many people would greet this trend and such a dramatic exponential curve as the best possible news, representing an enormous stimulation of the global economy with increasing products, services, markets, and consumers. Modern societies with capitalist economies have proven exceptionally adept at turning profusion into huge global pots of gold.

Fallenness—There exists a universal tendency for things to go wrong, a flaw that in theological terms is called fallenness. Nothing in the world or in all human experience is one hundred percent pure.

When we apply this law of fallenness to the concept of profusion, we see that fallenness exerts it own unique pull on every aspect of profusion. Just as no object on the earth's surface escapes the pull of gravity, so no object in a fallen world escapes the pull of fallenness.

Fallenness exists in either actualized or potential form. No matter which component of profusion we select or which product of progress we isolate, we can demonstrate how fallenness either *is* (actualized fallenness) or *can be* (potential fallenness) associated with it. Therefore, as the profusion curve rises rapidly, of necessity the fallenness associated with profusion also rises rapidly.

A Profusion of Positive—If we were to split the profusion graph into two components—the positive resulting from profusion and the negative resulting from profusion—we would notice that both of these component curves are growing rapidly. We would, in fact, have created two new "baby" exponential curves.

However, because most of what progress brings us is beneficial, we would notice that the graph of positive is growing faster than the negative. As a matter of fact, *far* faster. Thus the general optimism of many observers in the world—that things are rapidly getting better—seems not only accurate and well placed but also reassuring.

A Profusion of Negative—Of course we are still left with the curve of negative that must be dealt with. As we think of profusion, we must remember that nothing in this world is pure and that everything is affected in some way by fallenness. Even as the positive is growing at an astounding exponential rate, we see that the negative is also growing at an exponential rate, although admittedly not as dramatically as the positive.

Separate Accounting of Good and Bad—Because we have both the positive curve and the negative curve, it is important for us to understand how to think about these two commodities. Our usual tendency in assessing good versus bad is to use a fairly standard accounting method. For this, we do a simple subtraction of the bad from the good and see if we have a balance left over. If we have a net balance resulting, we call this a profit. If on a consistent basis we acquire enough profit, we take it as an indication that things are getting better, that life is improving, that we are "progressing." If we were to apply this same accounting process to progress and profusion, we would indeed see more good than bad, that is, a net positive balance.

Unfortunately, progress has thrown us a curve. In our contemporary situation with progress it is important to realize that the negative must be accounted separately, because *if the negatives are sufficiently dangerous, they cannot be offset by the positives no matter how beneficial the positives are.* Although we are not accustomed to calculating this way, it is important that we learn to do so, for there are no exemptions granted for ignorance.

Threshold of Lethality—Beyond calculating the good and the bad separately, we now need to examine one additional component of the negative: lethality. Once a certain critical mass of negative has accumulated, it will reach the threshold of lethality. At this point, the entire system will be doomed, *no matter how much positive has been compiled.* It makes no difference if we have ten units of good, a thousand units, or a trillion units. Lethality will still win.

That such a potential threshold of lethality exists for the world system is undeniable. The only uncertainty comes in assessing how far into the future such a threshold lies, how long it will take for us to reach this threshold, and if there is anything that can be done to prevent us from colliding with it. But from a mathematical point of view, we are approaching it at a very rapid speed—and continuously accelerating.

To summarize:

- The world is always—and unavoidably—experiencing an increased *profusion*.
- With each new level of profusion we have much new positive but, unavoidably in a fallen world, *we also have much new negative*.
- The growth of positive is rapid, approximating exponential growth. But *the corresponding growth of negative is also alarmingly rapid*.
- Once this quantum, this critical mass, of negative reaches a certain *threshold of lethality*, it will prove fatal for our world system.
- *No amount of positive can offset this negative and the impending lethality*.
- We have no possible option but to continue in this fatal direction because of our total dependency on progress.

Because this is a conceptual model, it cannot predict exactly how lethality will exert itself. Nor can it predict when. And the thesis of this book *does not presume to make such predictions*. But this much is clear—the accumulation of negative is exponential. And that can go on for only so long before the entire system collapses under the weight of its damage.

A WORD ABOUT SPEED

I have warned repeatedly about the dramatic nature of exponential change. Still, this effect will be underestimated. Under conditions of exponentiality, change can go from almost undetectable to overwhelming in the blink of an eye. And, I fear, this is precisely the speed with which the scenario for the end of the age will play itself out.

Let's illustrate the drama involved through one final example of exponential change. The Pacific Ocean spans sixty-four million square miles and, on average, is 14,000 feet deep. If all the continents of the world were placed inside it, there would still be room for another Asia.

Question: Assume that the Pacific dried up and it was our job to fill it. If we began with a single drop of water and continued doubling the amount, how many doublings would be necessary to refill the ocean?

Answer: Eighty.

Question: How full is the ocean at the seventieth doubling?

Answer: Less than one-tenth of one percent.

The implications should be apparent. If the thesis outlined here is conceptually correct, the collapse will happen in the last fraction of time.

DOES THE WORLD SYSTEM HAVE CANCER?

Perhaps the process of cancer is a helpful illustration to summarize the flow of the above argument. When the first cancer cells develop, they make absolutely no difference to the functioning of the trillions of other cells within the body. Each of these other cells continues to carry on its work in a healthy manner while ignoring the presence of the few malignant cells. This is the pre-morbid, subclinical stage.

But cancer cells grow—and their growth is exponential. Soon these abnormal cells reach a mass whereby symptoms begin to manifest themselves. Not death, but dysfunction. This is the symptomatic stage.

Still, the cancer cells do not stop there. They continue to grow and divide. And once they reach the lethal stage, the entire body succumbs. Perhaps the cardiovascular, renal, gastrointestinal, and nervous systems are all still functioning normally. But if the lungs are consumed with malignancy, the entire body has a problem— we cannot live without oxygen.

To apply this illustration of cancer and the body to the situation of fallenness and the world, it is my estimation that the world system has already passed the pre-morbid state and is now in the symptomatic state. Even though not *all* of the world systems are at risk, such is not necessary. Lethality only has to choke off life from one essential system for the entire corpus to die.

BUT TAKE HEART!

Some look only at the graph of rapidly accumulating benefit, and they naturally want to celebrate the spectacular bounty of progress. Others look only at the graph of rapidly accumulating negative, and they naturally want to hide in the nearest cave. Both, I believe, miss the point.

These days are not about fear—they are about privilege. These days will not be dominated ultimately by the chaos of worldly forces but by the sovereignty of God. "I have told you these things, so that in me you may have peace," explained Jesus. "In this world you will have trouble. But take heart! I have overcome the world."[1]

It is time to start living as if we believed it.

CHAPTER NINE

THE TRIGGERING OF LETHALITY

Precise dates and details for the end of the age cannot be predicted, and thus it is the *process* previously outlined that should dominate our attention. Nevertheless, several issues present themselves as clear candidates and prominent players in the dramatic saga unfolding before us.

In this chapter we will examine specific trends that will most likely play a significant role in our impending future disruption. First we will consider those issues that have sufficient power and virulence to cause global lethality. Secondly, we will look at those triggering issues which, while perhaps not dealing the final blow, might nevertheless play an important role in setting the stage.

LETHAL WEAPONS

Within the context of the evidence presented in this book, there are four major issues that have the potential of bringing down the final curtain on the world system: war, weapons of mass destruction (the use of which is not limited to the context of a defined war), infectious pandemics, and ecocatastrophes. Each of these issues is affected by progress, profusion, irreversibility, exponentiality, and fallenness—in the same way that a bonfire is affected by pine branches and gasoline.

War

"The world in which we live," lamented Bertrand Russell, "has been shaped by some 6,000 years of organized warfare."[1] Violence and war have consistently characterized human activity from the beginning. "It is deeply disturbing to realize that in fifty-five centuries of recorded history there have been only 292 years of 'peace,'" explains William Goetz in *Apocalypse Next*. "Furthermore, mankind has never yet fashioned a weapon that hasn't been used."[2] A worrisome fact indeed when we stop to consider that world military spending is eight hundred billion dollars annually. That kind of money can buy a lot of global damage.

The twentieth century experienced two world wars in which more than sixty million people perished—a level of carnage unimaginable in any previous century. Thankfully, international negotiations have, to date, avoided a third world war. But replacing such large-scale conflicts has been an endless series of terrorism, Jihad, micro-wars, and irregular warfare. Since 1945, there has been continuous warfare somewhere on the planet, with no indication that this type of violent activity will diminish.

Future battles will develop faster and require fewer soldiers, but will use more technology and weaponry with greater lethality. "In the future the shelf life of victory will be short," says Roger Spiller, professor of military history at the Army's futuristic Fort Leavenworth. "Military operations will proliferate but mean less."[3] Colonel Thomas Suitt, who runs a command-preparation course, explains how tank battle commanders will have four hundred vehicles and five thousand soldiers to lead against similar forces in a "combat window" where all will be decided in fifteen to thirty minutes.[4]

Of great concern is the prominent role missile technology plays in the destabilization of our collective future. Most Americans do not realize what is at stake in this critical dimension of the global equation. To maximally threaten their enemies, terrorist entities—whether nations or organizations—require four components:

- Money to develop or purchase weaponry
- Warheads—conventional, nuclear, biological, or chemical
- Missile technology to shoot such warheads over the required distances
- The political will to do so

Most terrorists groups and rogue nations lack only the missile technology. Yet many such groups with nefarious motives are rapidly developing ballistic capability or buying it through technology transfer. Once such a missile is enroute, there is no way to prevent it reaching the target. With luck, guidance systems might prove erratic. But the commonly held idea that it can be shot down is largely naive.

A commission granted unprecedented access to CIA secrets about the foreign missile threat to American territory concluded that Iran could build a ballistic missile capable of an attack on New York City by 2003.[5] Similar concerns are harbored about the military activities of North Korea, China, Iraq, Syria, Pakistan, and the republics of the former Soviet Union—all of which have been known to traffic in the transfer of sensitive missile technology. Once such strike capacity exists, what is to prevent a hotheaded, desperate, mentally unstable, religiously fanatical megalomaniac from pushing the fateful button?

Syndicated columnist William Safire described this Arab doomsday scenario: "Say a future Iraq moves on Kuwait again. The U.S. prepares to liberate the victim, but then the aggressor claims to have a missile aimed at Chicago. When the U.S. President warns Iraq of total annihilation, the dictator shrugs it off as his way to Heaven. The CIA estimates the chances at seventy percent that he is faking—but if he is not, there would go Chicago."[6]

At a recent National Security Seminar, one speaker commented: "In comparison to the present, in some ways it seems like the Cold War was a piece of cake."[7] Many are surprised by such views. But it is time to face the truth of a dangerously fallen, fully militarized, increasingly fanatical world. Robert D. Kaplan, a brilliant global observer, worries about that increasingly large and destitute segment of world population who "find war and a barracks existence a step up rather than a stop down."[8] Adds military expert David Tucker: "A realistic assessment of the world into which we are moving accepts the possibility that terrible things may await us."[9]

"After every war everyone declared the end of war," comments Fort Leavenworth's Colonel Jerry Morelock. "Though now we talk about lots of smaller wars, what's to prevent a really big conflagration? The record of history indicates that a new and great threat is certain."[10]

Weapons of Mass Destruction

Weapons of mass destruction (WMD) continue to represent one of the gravest threats to world stability and indeed to world viability. Any end-of-the-age scenario will, in all likelihood, involve their use in some capacity. WMD generally refers to three possibilities: nuclear weapons, biological weapons, and chemical weapons. Although nuclear weapons receive most attention, biological and chemical weapons are cheaper, easier, and require less technological sophistication. Because of these significant advantages, they are attractive options for poor but fanatical players in the arena of global violence.

Former Senator Sam Nunn provided this assessment of American vulnerabilities: "Libyan terrorists launch a drone airplane bearing canisters of deadly anthrax microbes into the Capitol as the

President is delivering his State of the Union Address to Congress. . . . Or North Korea succeeds in developing nuclear weapons and is poised to attack South Korea, where 37,000 U.S. troops are stationed. Or Iraq rebuilds its chemical weapons arsenal and fires nerve gas into Kuwait aboard Scud missiles."[11]

Harry Cohen in *The Brown Journal of World Affairs* outlines the frightening convergence of global threats that plague our day: the proliferation of weapons of mass destruction, state fragmentation, and terrorism. "In the past, it was acceptable to consider these threats separately," explains Cohen. "To do so now, however, would be to ignore the gravity of a global problem unique to our era. . . . What is it about this period in our existence that has allowed these threats to converge? Transnationalism, the existence of the most lethal weapons humankind has ever known, and the confusion and turmoil that accompany structural change in the international system have combined to *create a global environment unlike any previously experienced by humankind,* and this environment has facilitated the convergence of threats."[12] [emphasis mine]

Nuclear weapons have contributed to global hyperacidity ever since the atomic genie escaped its bottle on August 6, 1945 in Hiroshima. It took Russia exactly four years to construct its own A-bomb. The United States and Russia continue to hold ninety-six percent of the world's nuclear weapons. The essence of the nuclear difficulty we face today arises basically from two sources: (1) nations wishing to develop or augment a nuclear arsenal for purposes of national defense or pride; and (2) nuclear leakage resulting from the breakup of the former Soviet Union and the potentially lucrative black market in nuclear technology. As a result of these two threats, the United States spends $67 million *per day* preparing for the possibility of nuclear war.[13]

Our deterrent strategy with the former Soviet Union relied on the policy of Mutually Assured Destruction (MAD). Because, as already mentioned, there is no defensive system capable of preventing missiles from landing within our borders, we had to depend on the deterrent of assuring the complete annihilation of our attacker. The MAD deterrence worked under the conditions of the Cold War when it was a bipolar standoff. But there is no guarantee that such a policy can work in the highly uncertain world of the post-Cold War era.

"Those of us who spent our formative years during the halcyon days of the Cold War cannot escape feeling a modicum of nostalgia for the simplicity of that era," remarks defense expert Tarek E. Masoud. "While the bipolar structure of the Cold War nuclear confrontation ensured its stability, the chaos of the post-Cold War era has seen Third World 'rogue' states—like Iraq and North Korea—and possibly even terrorist elements become the newest players in an increasingly volatile nuclear game. Since everyone with an ax to grind appears to be trying to acquire nuclear materials, it seems inevitable that eventually someone, somewhere will succeed. . . . How does the West deter non-state terrorist actors with nuclear bombs and nothing to lose?"[14]

The former USSR developed hundreds of metric tons of highly enriched uranium and plutonium, currently stockpiled at various sites. According to nuclear authority James Doyle, experts "now realize that the scope of the nuclear materials security problem within the former Soviet nuclear complex is much larger than was estimated when the original plans were formulated in 1994. At that time, the U.S. government estimated that approximately 80-100 facilities at several dozen sites . . . contained weapons-usable nuclear materials. However, by early 1998, the Department of Energy had identified over 150 facilities at 53 sites containing such materials or related to their security."[15]

Large quantities of weapons-usable nuclear materials in the former Soviet Union remain inadequately secured. Once stolen or sold on the black market, the threat is real. Nuclear weapons expert Graham T. Allison emphasizes four concerns:

- Once fissile material is available, weaponization is easy. The denial of access to fissile material is the only reliable means of denying access to nuclear weapons.

- Transportation is easy. The simplest bomb design can be made with less than twenty pounds of plutonium—weights that could be physically carried by a single human being.
- Delivery against the United States is easy. America has borders that are exceptionally porous. The means of delivery into or against the United States are essentially infinite.
- Demand exists. Many entities are interested in acquiring this capacity.

Conclusion: It is only a matter of time before such weapons are used—even against the United States, and possibly within our borders. "Suppose that instead of mini-vans filled with hundreds of pounds of the crude explosives used in Oklahoma City and New York, terrorists had acquired a suitcase carrying one hundred pounds of highly enriched uranium roughly the size of a grapefruit," illustrates Allison. "Using a simple, well known design to build a weapon from this material, terrorists could have produced a nuclear blast equivalent to 10,000 to 20,000 tons of TNT. Under normal conditions, this would devastate a three-square-mile urban area. Much of Oklahoma City would have disappeared. The tip of Manhattan, including all of Wall Street would have been destroyed."[16]

Although a catastrophic rupture of the Russian nuclear complex into international black markets has not yet taken place, experts warn that there have been known cases of theft or illicit trafficking in fissile material. What's more, it is likely to continue and could easily get worse. The deep and systemic internal disorders of Russian society today are a frightening matter of public record.[17]

Many countries and terrorist organizations are credible nuclear threats. The recent tests by India and Pakistan seriously upped the ante in the Asian subcontinent. Both countries now possess both nuclear weapons and ballistic missiles—plus long-standing animosity and distrust. Since missiles could reach their targets in ten minutes, warns one White House aide, "you have a situation where either side, thinking its forces may be under attack, would launch on warning." Without satellites, the warning systems for each country are not dependable. It's a hair-trigger situation in which miscalculation could easily lead to a nuclear exchange.[18]

"A nuclear detonation in the atmosphere that is not a test is probable in the next ten to fifteen years," says Roger Spiller, the George C. Marshall Professor of Military History at Leavenworth, "if only because groups, as well as rogue states, will be acquiring the technology without also acquiring the diplomatic skills and bureaucratic control mechanisms for keeping a nuke without miscalculating."[19]

Says Cohen, "The destructive capacity of weaponry has been increasing exponentially throughout this century. Quite simply, humans are capable of killing other humans in greater numbers and more quickly than ever before."[20]

Biological weapons are another serious WMD threat, with anthrax being the agent most feared. Anthrax, normally a disease of sheep or goats, is weaponized by releasing airborne spores for people to breathe. Once inhaled, it is ninety-nine percent lethal. Within a few days cold-like symptoms develop. By the time these symptoms occur, treatment is too late. Death ensues within a week.

The Department of Defense asserts that anthrax is in the developing weapons arsenal of at least ten nations. "It's the poor man's atomic bomb," says Rear Admiral Michael Cowan, deputy director for the Joint Chiefs of Staff. "It's ubiquitous. It's everywhere. It's easy to get ahold of. It's easy to grow." Although to date, anthrax has yet to be used in warfare, the U.S. military now requires vaccination of all troops.[21]

Smallpox and plague are additional infectious agents prompting concern. Russian defectors have given unconfirmed reports of yet other biological "super-plague" organisms that the Soviets were developing—diseases with *no known antidotes* in the Western world.

Chemical weapons are technically more difficult than biological weapons yet quite easy in comparison to nuclear weapons. Saddem Hussein, for example, had chemical weapons during the Gulf War. And in 1995, the terrorist Aum Shinrikyo cult exposed thousands of Tokyo subway commuters to the sarin nerve agent. Twelve died in this attack and approximately 5,000 were injured.

"The threat or use of nuclear-biological-chemical weapons is a likely condition of future warfare," warns a strategy outline drafted for the *Quadrennial Defense Review*.[22] Murphy's Law of Human Behavior holds: *If something bad can be done, ultimately, someone bad will do it.*

Infectious Pandemics—Infectious disease does not require human weaponry to do its damage—any passive, unwitting human host will serve nicely. There was a time in our not-so-distant past when we haughtily thought total victory against infectious illness was possible. Today we know better. Fully one-third of all deaths worldwide are from infectious diseases.

We have, of course, achieved great success through public health, sanitation, immunizations, and antibiotics. But to declare victory is foolish. In 1980, for example, I had never heard of HIV or Lyme disease, and I was barely aware of *Chlamydia*. A decade later, we had a global AIDS pandemic killing millions, Wisconsin was in the middle of Lyme disease hysteria, and *Chlamydia* was the leading sexually transmitted disease, infecting four and a half million Americans annually.

In 1995, *The Journal of the American Medical Association* and thirty-two other medical journals worldwide dedicated an entire edition to emergent infectious diseases. With ten million people crossing international boundaries daily, the stage is set for rapidly spreading outbreaks. Bacteria and viruses do not carry passports and do not check in with customs agents as they pass from country to country. Virtually all infectious diseases known have incubation periods long enough for a person to be exposed to the illness and then travel anywhere in the world before becoming ill.

The 1918 influenza pandemic killed eighteen million people worldwide. What is to prevent a similar even more virulent virus from spreading globally today? Smallpox could kill millions if not billions should it somehow resurface on our planet. Ebola virus is extremely deadly. Hanta virus can result in fatal respiratory infection after only a few minutes exposure in a laboratory where it is being studied.

We now realize that once the stage is set, there are latent infectious diseases waiting to make their presence known. What will be the new millennium's equivalent to today's HIV? Is it possible that an infectious Armageddon might await us? "If we allow ourselves to contaminate our planetary home, we will produce the conditions required for our disintegration or extermination," writes futurist Melville C. Branch. "This could occur if the atmosphere carried radioactive contamination from a war or nuclear accident around the world. But the possibility of a deadly pandemic from an unknown organism is much greater—particularly if it is airborne or cannot be successfully quarantined—because of the continuous transportation of more and more people, goods, and services far and wide throughout the world."[23]

Ecocatastrophe

For decades, scientists have publicly worried that the human race is actively committing global suicide via environmental degradation—a kind of slithering-down death by ecocide. We are testing the limits of ecosystem resilience in a way never before attempted, with no assurance of long-term survival.

Global warming currently gets the most press, but there are dozens of other issues vying for top of the leader board: desertification, deforestation, population growth, topsoil depletion, rivers that are "too thin to plow and too thick to drink," holes in the ozone, anoxic oceanic "dead zones," species extinction, resource depletion, oil spills, nuclear power plant accidents, hazardous waste pits oozing toxic and radioactive slime into the underworld. We are hitting the hive with a stick, and the bees are plotting their revenge.

Global temperatures are reportedly rising in response to rising atmospheric carbon dioxide levels—which have increased every decade since the Industrial Revolution. If trends continue, glaciers and polar caps will increasingly melt, ocean levels will rise, currents will change, heat waves and deserts will increase, and all those Midwesterners who want ocean frontage might get their wish.

Species extinction is reported at a rate one thousand times faster than any time in history. Large sections of the great tropical rain forests are fighting for their lives. Over the last century, deserts have increased 150 percent. The weather is measurably stormier— and certainly seems apocalyptic to me.

"Man eats up nature," accused Francis Schaeffer in *Pollution and the Death of Man.*[24] A generic formula for environmental damage is *population × affluence × technology*. When we factor in exponentially . . . it seems like Schaeffer had it right.

TRIGGERING ISSUES

Economics

Who can doubt that if we experience a terminal event, economics will be found somewhere in the middle of the final scrimmage? Electronic money is flying around the globe like mad, and the resultant levels of volatility are custom-made for crisis. International relations specialist Walter Russell Mead explains how it has been our expressed policy to make economic activity flow ever faster and unfettered. Yet, he warns, "The faster capitalism goes, the more dangerous it gets." His sober prediction about our current dangerous state of international economic plight: "It does not, frankly, take a rocket scientist to predict that this will all end in tears."[25]

Global economic integration leads to tight-coupling (a condition of extreme interdependence where linkages are inseparably connected). And tight coupling leads to falling dominos. As seizures pass through the world markets at the speed of light, even experts have lost the ability to predict—and it is unnerving. This year's "economic miracle" turns into next year's economic debacle—and nobody knows exactly why. The truly frightening part is how often these changes are not even considered in the realm of plausibility. "What happens in one part of the world eventually *will* affect everything," explains Jeffrey Garten, dean of the Yale School of Management. "But it might not be in the way that we expect, because the links are almost beyond human comprehension."[26]

Speaking of the Asian collapse in the late 1990s, one economist observed: "This is like an earthquake. You can hear all the rumblings and see the sensors telling you the plates are moving around. But no one can say what will trigger the earthquake or when it will hit or how much damage it will do."[27] Former Treasury Department official Roger Altman called the global capital markets "the Nuke of the 1990s," that, when arrayed against any nations, can impose "previously unthinkable changes."[28]

Politics

Perhaps nothing is more divisive in American life than political ideology: not religion, not race, not gender. We should therefore not be surprised to find the same level of conflict on an international scale.

Why, for example, would India be willing to incur sanctions and chill foreign investment by testing a nuclear device? "The simple explanation is politics," explained *Newsweek* columnist Fareed Zakaria. "With this one move, the Bharatiya Janata Party . . . has secured its future."[29] In a nation of nearly one billion people, ninety-one percent supported the decision. "The explosions animated the nation's spirits and boosted the new prime minister's political fortunes," observed columnist Bruce B. Auster. "Many Indians actually took pride in the fact that their leaders had poisoned relations with the United States and much of the rest of the world."[30]

What is true for India is no less true for scores of other politically fanatical nations. The politicization of Islam is surely one of the most dangerous trends in an out-of-control world. Israeli scholar and military adviser Yehezekel Dror warned of the "threat of crazy states that are driven by high-intensity aggressive ideologies." Dror mocked the "widespread views that progressing modernity will produce more rational international behavior," and argued that "confessional conflicts, holy wars, committed crusaders, and martyrdom-seeking warriors are not relics of the past, but the most pressing threats of the present. . . . The proliferation of weapons of mass destruction make these ideologies very dysfunctional, up to endangering the very survival of the human species."[31]

Religion

Throughout recorded human history, religion has always been a source of conflict—often armed deadly conflict. "Men never do evil so completely and cheerfully as when they do it from religious conviction," remarked French philosopher Blaise Pascal.

Although deeply held religious beliefs drive conflict on every continent, currently it is militant Islam that poses the greatest threat. "Beyond its stark, clearly articulated message, Islam's very militancy makes it attractive to the downtrodden," asserts Robert Kaplan. "It is the one religion that is *prepared to fight!*"[32] As a former high-ranking government official recently summarized, "If a group of Iranian mullahs one day has a very long range ballistic missile—and decides that not only they but all their countrymen can go to heaven if they just launch a nuclear weapon at the 'Great Satan'—that's not the kind of people deterrence would work against."[33]

Tribalism, Ethnicity, and Nationalism

The militant tendencies of tribalism, ethnicity, and nationalism are a clear matter of historical record. "Today there is no tribe, no faction or splinter group or neighborhood gang, that does not aspire to self-determination," writes political science professor Benjamin R. Barber.[34]

We see it in the Balkans, in Asia, in the Middle East. But it is perhaps nowhere more brutally on display than in Africa, where, for example, the Rwandan genocide claimed 800,000 innocent people. "Ethnicity is a powerful element in irregular warfare. Ethnic conflicts in Liberia, Rwanda, Burundi and elsewhere in Africa have led to appalling human and economic losses," explains Jeffrey B. White in the *American Intelligence Journal*.[35] "I saw a soldier point a bayonet at a pregnant woman and cut out her baby," reported a Liberian man. "I tell you, it's a tribal war. There are no ideas, no politics, just tribe."[36]

THE END

Many additional issues could appropriately be included in a chapter on this topic. I fully realize that *none of these issues are sufficient to make the case that the world is going to end.* They are merely presented as evidence that such a putative end is possible, and that such an end has plenty of weaponry from which to choose its own terminal event.

Simply stated, each of the following factors are increasing exponentially without any demonstrable commensurate diminution of the fallenness problem: the power of weaponry, technology, communications, information, mobility, money, speed, and population. You do the math and draw your own conclusions.

Are we then to collapse in despair, move to the mountains, install perimeter fences, stockpile ammo for our Uzis, and put Prozac in the water? Hardly. Our only hope is that God is still God—and that He's still interested. But then, that has always been our only hope. It's just that the conditions of the present are clarifying what progress has otherwise tempted us to forget.

CHAPTER TEN

THE END OF LIFE AS WE KNOW IT: THE BEGINNING OF LIFE AS WE KNOW IT SHOULD BE

As a result of the argument forwarded in this book, I am convinced that we must prepare ourselves for the possible consequences of increasingly dramatic future disruption. This is not to say that the days ahead are to be dreaded. On the contrary, if God is culminating history on my watch, then I count it a privilege to have been chosen to live in such an interesting era.

We do indeed live in a special time in history. When Abraham first crossed the Canaanite border and entered the Promised Land, that was a special moment. When Moses first knocked on Pharaoh's door and demanded, "Let my people go," that was a special moment. When an unusual star first migrated over a lonely Bethlehem stable two thousands years ago, that was a special moment. Even so, on our generational shift, it seems to me that this, too, is a special moment. None of these "special moments" was free of strife. But each represented an unprecedented turning point in the history of the world system, a turning point from which there was no turning back.[1]

I am not intending to take this "special moment" and unduly constrain it with specific dates. But I *am* intending to take this "special moment" and constrain it by association with a specific process: a process that is powerful, rapid, irreversible, and unprecedented. The exponential curve of profusion is real and very powerful. The pull of fallenness is real and very powerful. And, historically speaking, the speed with which it is happening is nothing short of breathtaking. The entire process is careening along at breakneck speed, yet continuously accelerating. I cannot foresee any interruption or intervention that will deliver us from the consequences of this process.

Progress is putting on a parade to dazzle the entire globe, and we are all enjoying the show. But, lurking in the shadows, fallenness is rapidly assembling its own parade. As long as the often subclinical ill effects of fallenness remain obscured by the spectacle of progress, we will be relatively inattentive. But once fallenness develops its own independent critical mass of power and speed, lethality will be the next destination.

ON LIVING READY

Does this all mean that we should quit our jobs and sit on a hilltop fatalistically waiting for the inevitable? Hardly. There is much to be done. And there is much to be made right.

This book is not at all about fatalism or desperation. It is a call to authenticity. Let me explain.

If death came today and knocked on our doors, most of us would be inclined to respond: "Give me a month to get ready." Get ready for what? To straighten out priorities? To begin living consistent with our beliefs? If *that* is what we need a month to prepare for, then why wait for death—or the end of the age? Why not get ready now? Why not *live* ready?

Warning signals of sufficient magnitude have a way of getting us started down such a path, of motivating us toward action in the direction we have known to be right all along. A heart attack, for example, often will get us off the couch and into the gym when nothing else worked. Coughing up blood will often shut down cigarettes in an instant.

Most of our days are spent in the stupor of routine, going down life's treadmill on autopilot. But a heart attack or cancer surgery — or a house fire, plane crash, or earthquake — has a way of helping us replace the stupor with something more authentic. In this sense, confronting the end of the age is an opportunity. It makes us look at the Big Picture and contemplate needed change. The thought of an imminent interview with the Almighty has a way of clarifying priorities in the direction of authenticity. It is a process that should not have to wait any longer.

AUTHENTICITY

Authenticity might be defined as the congruence between what we believe and how we live. Without authenticity there is neither integrity nor credibility. Without authenticity, if death came to knock we would need a month to get ready. One of the great gifts of authenticity, however, is that it leaves us continuously ready for whatever comes next. We live without regrets, purified by virtue and verity.

Let's examine four aspects of the fully authentic life that will help us live ready: vision, values, relationships, and lifestyle. If these four are in place, nothing in this book — or in the future — should be perceived as a threat.

An Authentic Vision

Vision has languished under the stressful and overloaded demands of our modern age. When dodging bullets on a nanosecond basis it is hard to feel in a visionary mood about the long haul. But vision is important for both direction and hope. Can we articulate a vision of authentic kingdom living that can transcend both our "chronic randomness" and the coming chaos?

A vision is not an arbitrary string of verbiage constructed to fill

a vacant morning at the corporate board retreat. It is the foundation
for our thoughts, actions, and values. Therefore, it is not enough to
have a vision—we must also *live* it. This is where authenticity
comes in.

As a part of this vision, we will see God clearly, understand that
He is good and that He is Love. We will understand that He is a
God who cares, who changes hearts, who redeems pain, and who
works in history. We will understand that He is drawing all people;
He is reconciling the world to Himself; He is building His church.
We will understand that He holds both our present and our future;
He has given us a foundation on which to stand that is unmovable
and unshakable.

As a part of our vision, we will understand that we are broken,
empty, and vulnerable, yet hopeful, redeemed, and thoroughly for-
given. We are ambassadors of reconciliation and witnesses, equipped
with truth and love, gifted with the Word, the Spirit, and the mind
of Christ.

As a part of our vision, we will commit to love the Lord, ourselves, and one another. We will seek first His kingdom. We will seek
to guard our unity and to resolve conflicts. We will seek to nourish
and protect relationships. We will seek to build the kingdom, telling
others the Good News with "gentleness and respect."

"Within the community whose hope is shaped by the biblical
story there is a clear vision of the goal of history—namely *the reconciliation of all things with Christ as head*—and the assurance that this
goal will be reached," explains theologian Lesslie Newbigin.[2] Such
a vision—and only such a vision—is capable of carrying us all the
way Home.

Authentic Values

"We need values because God has put in man an upward reach,"
explains Senator Gordon Humphrey. "Without values, nothing may
be thought virtuous. Without values, there is nothing against which

to measure performance or right and wrong or truth and falsehood. Without values, there are no standards."3 But what values and whose standards? Values must have a reference point, for as any sailor knows, "Without a destination, there is never a favorable wind."

In Heaven values will be unambiguous. In contrast, our current relativism has created a destination-free values frontier with no real reference point—and no real authenticity. A kind of values "duty-free shop" for international travel anywhere in the moral cosmos. Values-free relativism leads to a vacuum which, as Saul Bellow explains, "is a kind of ghost town into which anyone can move and declare himself sheriff."4

Values as a moving target has now been normalized for many "psychic whiplashed" victims of modernity. "Permanent flexibility," for example, is now called an "essential survival ethic in the Chaos Age" by futurist authors Jim Taylor and Watts Wacker. Due to the enormous level of "values dislocation" experienced in modern times, these authors recommend we find meaning in such a world by abandoning "the search for unifying theories."5 Sounds to me like trying to improve the farm by burning the crops and shooting the cows.

It is obvious to most Christian observers that the modern quest for authenticity in values has a problem—more accurately, at least three problems:

- The value structure of this world is very powerful— almost dictatorial.
- The value structure of this world is almost always in variance with the value structure found in the Scriptures— often polar opposite.
- The value structure of this world shifts in rapid and chaotic ways, almost as if it has no reference point whatsoever.

God, as always, is willing to lend a hand in helping us sort it all out. For millennia, He has been patiently trying to explain to us (not always an easy task) the radical difference between the value structure of His kingdom and that of this world. Power, money, career, education, status, and possessions, for example, assume a dominant role in our modern values hierarchy. But God takes each of these and reassigns a different value according to His eternal perspective. In such matters, God's definitions have a way of outlasting ours.

John Calvin suggests the first duty of the Christian is to make the invisible kingdom visible.[6] What then are the values of this invisible kingdom? For starters, there is peace, service, joy, lowliness, meekness, humility, forgiveness, compassion, reconciliation, brokenness, kindness, gentleness, grace, patience, self-control, submission, mercy, forbearance, wisdom, and unity. Finally, there is faith, hope, and love. It doesn't sound much like our world. But it does sound like the beginning of life as we know it should be.

Authentic Relationships

If on our death beds we were given an opportunity to re-roll the videotape and do one aspect of our lives over, what area would we pick? Most of us, I am convinced, would pick our relationships — the chance to improve our connections with those we love the most. Indeed, loving relationships are the mandate of eternity, and we neglect them at the peril of not only our happiness but also our testimony.

Love is not the road to authenticity — it *is* authenticity. Love is not just a good idea — it is the *only* idea. Love is not just the first step — it is the alpha and the omega.

To love is the central commandment of all eternity. To love God, ourselves, and our neighbors should be the first guideline for all life decisions and actions. Until we love, we are not permitted to go any further. If love is not right, nothing that follows can be right. Without it we are nothing, and we gain nothing. Christ's Great Commandment reduces to one concept: love. Love must precede all else. Secondary emotions may follow, but love is not expected to coexist with other feelings or actions. Instead, all other feelings and actions must coexist with love. If they cannot, they must go. There is no spiritually authentic aspect of living that does not include love.

Authenticity, then, means that we cherish, nourish, and protect our relationships: to God, to self, to others. Such relational authenticity, based on the truth of Scripture and the love of God, will survive the fire to come and will transcend the end of the age without fear.

Authentic Lifestyle

Authenticity suggests that we arrange our lives in such a way that when we cross into eternity there will be little to change. In practical terms, this requires that our day-to-day activities and behaviors be Christlike. Instead, we have settled for worldlike—yet seem scarcely aware we have been co-opted. "Somehow there has been a blending of the 'Christian lifestyle' with the lifestyle of this generation," observes former Navigator Missions leader, George Sanchez. "More and more the line of distinction is being rubbed out between the people of the kingdom of God and the people who know nothing of His kingdom. Many of the values of an unbelieving society . . . are becoming the same values of those who call themselves Christians. The dangerous thing about this is that it happens so imperceptibly."[7]

The call to Christlikeness is not a call to be weird. But it is a plea to be different if authenticity requires it. "To be a witness does not consist in engaging in propaganda or even in stirring people up, but in being a living mystery," explains Cardinal Suhard. "It means to live in such a way that one's life would not make sense if God did not exist."[8]

■ ■ ■

We can't con God. He knows if we are being fully authentic in our vision, values, relationships, and lifestyle—or if we are simply acting as cultural moderns addicted to progress. There is a difference.

This, then, is what authenticity means to me: that condition of complete integrity where the difference between our testimony and our lives is too small to be measured. In the interesting and challenging days ahead, it is not enough to coast along and be "approximately" Christian. We must reexamine everything and be "exactly" Christian.

NEVER DESPAIR

It is a great day for faith. Yes, perhaps the twilight of a great era is upon us. Perhaps the road ahead will carry us through unprecedented disruption and suffering. Nevertheless, God's kingdom is on the move in a powerful, unstoppable way. The gates of hell will not prevail. The outcome of the cosmic battle is already known. The opportunities for ministry have never been greater.

A certain amount of frustration is inevitable. But there is no need to despair. Every day, 250,000 more people are added to the world's population. And every day, 70-100,000 are added to the church's population as *intentional* believers (as opposed to nominal believers). Intentional Christianity is exponentially increasing in both the percentage of world population and also absolute numbers. In many countries, the kingdom is simply exploding with growth. Every week, thousands of new churches are born. The Gospel has been translated into the 2,000[th] language, and mission authorities are talking about the "finishable task." For the first time, there is "light at the end of the Great Commission tunnel."

Our vision is staggeringly comprehensive. Our weapons are truth and love. Our inheritance is incorruptible. Nothing can separate us from the love of God. We are the only ones in a ravaged society who have a sure foundation on which to stand.

God's ways are vindicated in every social experiment ever conducted. His advice always turns out to be the healthy option. We have assurance that our biggest problem—larger than all our other problems added together and multiplied by infinity—has been solved. We know forgiveness, we know grace, we know hope. We know love, we know truth, we know the Cross, and we know the Savior of the Cross. What a privilege to be picked to live today!

In 1935, philosopher Nicolas Berdyaev, having been expelled from Russia and writing in Paris, witnessed the cataclysmic beginning of World War II. Europe had continued in turmoil since the end of World War I, and then in 1933, Hitler had come to power in Germany. It was a time made for somber prophets. Within the context of this war-threatened setting, Berdyaev's observations about the Christian faith serve to both warn and encourage us today.

"A new day is dawning for Christianity in the world. . . . The hour has struck when, after terrible struggle, after an unprecedented de-Christianization of the world and its passage through all the results of that process, Christianity will be revealed in its pure form. Then it will be clear what Christianity stands for and what it stands against. Christianity will again become the only and the final refuge of man. And when the purifying process is finished, it will be seen that Christianity stands for man and for humanity, for the value and dignity of personality, for freedom, for social justice, for the brotherhood of men and of nations, for enlightenment, for the creation of a new life. And it will be clear that only Christianity stands for these things. The judgment upon Christianity is really judgment upon the betrayal of Christianity."9

Ours is the opportunity to stand for something. Or ours is the indictment of betrayal.

If Christ is even now saddling His horse to return, may He find us faithful.

NOTES

PREFACE

1. C. S. Lewis, "Is Progress Possible?" *God in the Dock: Essays on Theology and Ethics* (Grand Rapids, MI: Eerdmans, 1970), page 312.
2. John Maddox, *The Doomsday Syndrome* (New York, NY: McGraw-Hill Book Company, 1972), page 3.
3. Bruce Page, "Analyzing the Future," in *Living in the Future*, Isaac Asimov, editor (New York, NY: Beaufort Books, 1985), page 18.

CHAPTER 1—AN INTRODUCTION TO THE FUTURE WE MIGHT NOT HAVE

1. Edward Wenk, Jr., quoting Alfred North Whitehead, *Tradeoffs: Imperatives of Choice in a High-Tech World* (Baltimore: The Johns Hopkins University Press, 1986), page 202.
2. Alfred Kazin, "Cry, the Beloved Country," *Forbes-75th Anniversary Issue*, 14 September 1992, pages 140 and 144.

3. Richard Kyle, quoting Michael Grosso, *The Last Days Are Here Again: A History of the End Times* (Grand Rapids, MI: Baker House, 1998), page 191.

4. Bertrand Russell, *Has Man a Future?* (Baltimore, MD: Penguin Books, 1961), page 69.

5. Russell, page 70.

6. John W. Whitehead, quoting Lewis Thomas, *The End of Man* (Westchester, IL: Crossway Books, 1986), page 71.

7. Carl Sagan, *Cosmos* (New York, NY: Random House, 1980), page 328.

8. William R. Goetz, quoting Dr. George Walk, *Apocalypse Next: The End of Civilization as We Know It?* (Camp Hill, PA: Horizon Books, 1996), page 15.

9. Goetz, quoting Tom Harper, page 28.

10. Margaret Mead, "Models and Systems Analyses as Metacommunication," in *The World System: Models, Norms, Variations*, Ervin Laszlo, editor (New York, NY: George Braziller, 1973), page 27.

11. Alvin Toffler, *The Third Wave* (New York, NY: Bantam Books, 1980), page 12.

12. Edward O. Wilson, "Is Humanity Suicidal?" *The New York Times Magazine*, 30 May 1993, page 27.

13. Melville C. Branch, "Why We Simulate Long-range Futures," *The Futurist*, April 1998, page 52.

14. Russell, page 120.

15. William Strauss and Neil Howe, *The Fourth Turning: An American Prophecy* (New York, NY: Broadway Books, 1997), page 6.

16. Strauss and Howe, page 330.

17. James Redfield, "Other Predictions for the Turn of the Millennium," *Signs of the Times*, October 1997, page 5.

18. Andrew Murr, "The End Is Nigh—But When Exactly Is Nigh?" *Newsweek*, 8 September 1997, page 12.

19. Ken Wade, "Year of Destiny?" *Signs of the Times*, October 1997, pages 3-5 and 29.

20. Goetz, page 47.

21. Kyle, page 152.

22. "No one knows about that day or hour, not even the angels in heaven, nor the Son, but only the Father. Be on guard! Be alert! You do not know when that time will come" (Mark 13:32-33).

23. A. J. Conyers, "Antichrist, Our Contemporary," *Books & Culture,* May/June 1996, page 9.

24. C. S. Lewis, *The World's Last Night and Other Essays* (New York, NY: Harcourt Brace Jovanovich, 1960), pages 100-101.

25. "Update: A 1997 U.S.News & World Report Poll," *Signs of the Times,* August 1998, page 7.

26. Jeffery L. Sheler, "The Christmas Covenant," *U.S.News & World Report,* 19 December 1994, page 62.

27. Luke 17:26-30.

28. Lewis, page 107.

CHAPTER 2—PROFUSION THROUGH PROGRESS

1. Roberto Vacca, *The Coming Dark Age,* translated by J. S. Whale (Garden City, NY: Anchor Books, 1974), page 6.

2. "Vital Statistics," *Hippocrates,* May 1998, page 12.

3. Warren C. Robinson, "Global Population Trends," *Resources,* Spring 1998, Issue 131, pages 6-9.

4. Bill McKibben, "A Special Moment in History," *The Atlantic Monthly,* May 1998, pages 55, 60.

5. David Shenk, *Data Smog: Surviving the Information Glut* (New York, NY: HarperEdge, 1997), page 30.

6. Jim Taylor and Watts Wacker, with Howard Means, *The 500-Year Delta: What Happens After What Comes Next* (New York, NY: HarperBusiness, 1996), page 151.

7. George Gilder, "Happy Birthday *Wired:* It's Been a Weird Five Years," *Wired,* January 1998, page 40.

8. Alvin and Heidi Toffler, "Preparing for Conflict," *The Futurist,* June/July 1998, pages 26-29.

9. Barry Asmus, economist, presenting for Dain Bosworth Lecture, Rockford, IL, June 1997.

10. McKibben, page 55.

CHAPTER 3—THE IRREVERSIBILITY OF PROGRESS

1. Kenneth E. Boulding, *The Meaning of the Twentieth Century: The Great Transition* (New York, NY: Harper & Row, 1964), pages 186 and 191.
2. Alvin Toffler, *Future Shock* (New York, NY: Bantam, 1970), page 428.
3. Herman Kahn, William Brown, and Leon Martel, *The Next 200 Years: A Scenario for America and the World* (New York, NY: Morrow, 1976), page 165.
4. Daniel J. Boorstin, *The Discoverers* (New York, NY: Random House, 1983), page 271.
5. Boulding, page 23.
6. Boorstin, page 488.

CHAPTER 4—THE PHENOMENON OF EXPONENTIAL GROWTH

1. Paul R. Ehrlich, *The Population Bomb* (New York, NY: Ballantine Books, 1968), page 18.
2. Ehrlich, page 66.
3. Ehrlich, page 196.
4. Richard A. Falk, *This Endangered Planet: Prospects and Proposals for Human Survival* (New York, NY: Vintage Books, 1971), pages xi and 4.
5. Falk, page 27.
6. Falk, page 212.
7. Dennis Meadows, et al., *The Limits to Growth* (New York, NY: Universe Books, 1972), page 25.
8. Meadows, page 71.
9. Meadows, page 183.
10. Richard A. Falk, quoting Jay Forrester, "Reforming World Order: Zones of Consciousness and Domains of Action," in *The World System: Models, Norms, Variations*, Ervin Laszlo, editor (New York, NY: George Braziller, Inc., 1973), page 82.
11. Ervin Laszlo, editor, *The World System*, page v.
12. Ervin Laszlo, "Uses and Misuses of World Systems Models," in *The World System*, page 3.

13. Roberto Vacca, *The Coming Dark Age: What Will Happen When Modern Technology Breaks Down?* (Garden City, NY: Anchor Books, 1974), page 4.

14. Vacca, page 8.

15. Vacca, page 10.

16. Vacca, page 14.

17. Herman Kahn, William Brown, and Leon Martel, *The Next 200 Years: A Scenario for America and the World* (New York, NY: William Morrow and Company, Inc., 1976), pages 26 and 27.

18. Kahn, Brown, Martel, page 27.

19. Kahn, Brown, Martel, page 173.

20. Jeremy Rifkin, *Entropy: A New World View* (New York, NY: Bantam Books, 1980), page 83.

21. A centillion is 10^{303}. A trillion is, as you know, 10^{12}. A trillion centillion is therefore a playful 10^{315}.

22. Richard L. Garwin, "The Technology of Nuclear Weapons," *Arms Control Today*, November/December 1997, pages 6 and 7.

CHAPTER 5—THE FALLENNESS OF THE WORLD SYSTEM

1. John Ortberg, *The Life You've Always Wanted: Spiritual Disciplines for Ordinary People* (Grand Rapids, MI: Zondervan, 1997), page 188.

2. Richard A. Swenson, M.D., *Margin: Restoring Emotional, Physical, Financial, and Time Reserves to Overloaded Lives* (Colorado Springs, CO: NavPress, 1992), page 31.

3. Bob Goudzwaard, *Idols of Our Time*, translated by Mark Vander Vennen (Downers Grove, IL: InterVarsity), page 11.

4. Charles Colson, *Loving God* (Grand Rapids, MI: Zondervan), page 103.

5. C. S. Lewis, *God in the Dock: Essays on Theology and Ethics* (Grand Rapids, MI: Eerdmans, 1970), page 312.

CHAPTER 6— A PROFUSION OF NEGATIVE

1. It should be pointed out, however, that the growth in the number of prisoners and bankruptcies has increased even faster than population growth alone accounts for.

2. In biblical times, many people did live to advanced age. But remember that average life expectancy also has to account for those who died in infancy, in childbirth, from infectious diseases, and so on. When taken together, the *average* life expectancy at the time of Christ was indeed 21 years.

   The 1900 and 2000 figures are for the United States. For the world, the data is somewhat different: 1955–48 years; 1995–65 years (estimate).

CHAPTER 8—THEREFORE . . .

1. John 16:33.

CHAPTER 9—THE TRIGGERING OF LETHALITY

1. Bertrand Russell, *Has Man a Future?* (Baltimore, MD: Penguin Books, 1961), page 11.
2. William R. Goetz, *Apocalypse Next* (Camp Hill, PA: Horizon Books, 1996, first printing 1981), page 35.
3. Robert D. Kaplan, quoting Roger Spiller, "Fort Leavenworth and the Eclipse of Nationhood," *The Atlantic Monthly*, September 1996, page 86.
4. Kaplan, quoting Thomas Suitt, page 78.
5. Bruce Auster, "Should America Worry about Missiles Again?" *U.S. News & World Report*, 27 July 1998, page 25.
6. William Safire, "Anti-Missile Issue," *The New York Times*, 22 August 1996, page A25, cited in Janne Nolan and Mark Strauss, "The Rogue's Gallery," *The Brown Journal of World Affairs*, Winter/Spring 1997, Vol. IV, Issue 1, page 24.
7. The U.S. Army War College, Carlisle, PA, follows a policy of nonattribution for the National Security Seminar events.
8. Robert D. Kaplan, "The Coming Anarchy," *The Atlantic Monthly*, February 1994, page 72.
9. David Tucker, "Fighting Barbarians," *Parameters: US Army War College Quarterly*, Summer 1998, page 74.
10. Robert D. Kaplan, quoting Jerry Morelock, "Fort Leavenworth and the Eclipse of Nationhood," page 77.
11. Thomas W. Lippman, quoting Sam Nunn, "If Nonproliferation Fails, Pentagon Wants Counterproliferation

in Place," *Washington Post*, 15 May 1994, page A11, cited in Nolan and Strauss, page 22.

12. Harry Cohen, "Proliferation, Fragmentation, and Terrorism: A Disturbing Convergence of Threats," *The Brown Journal of World Affairs*, Winter/Spring 1997, Volume IV, Issue 1, page 54.

13. "Defense Monitor," *Center for Defense Information*, February 1997, cited in "Nuclear Notes," *Peace Research*, August 1997, Vol. 29, No. 3, page 5.

14. Tarek E. Masoud, "Stealing the Fire: Nuclearizing the Third World," *The Brown Journal of World Affairs*, Winter/Spring 1997, Volume IV, Issue 1, pages 17-18.

15. James E. Doyle, "Improving Nuclear Materials Security in the Former Soviet Union: Next Steps for the MPC&A Program," *Arms Control Today*, March 1998, pages 12-13.

16. Graham T. Allison, "The Number One Threat of Nuclear Proliferation Today: Loose Nukes from Russia," *The Brown Journal of World Affairs*, Winter/Spring 1997, Volume IV, Issue 1, page 65.

17. Allison, page 65.

18. Douglas Waller, "Enemies Go Nuclear," *Time*, 8 June 1998, pages 46-48.

19. Robert D. Kaplan, quoting Roger Spiller, "Fort Leavenworth and the Eclipse of Nationhood," page 80.

20. Cohen, page 58.

21. Laura Myers, "Pentagon to Begin Anthrax Shots," *Associated Press*, 14 August 1998, (Internet).

22. Richard J. Newman, "Getting Ready for the Wrong War," *U.S. News & World Report*, 12 May 1997, page 34.

23. Melville C. Branch, "Why We Simulate Long-range Futures," *The Futurist*, April 1998, page 52.

24. Francis A. Schaeffer, *Pollution and the Death of Man: A Christian View of Ecology* (London: Hodder and Stoughton, 1970), page 51.

25. Walter Russell Mead, "The Coming Economic Collapse," *Esquire*, October 1998, Volume 130, Number 4, page 97.

26. "Global Roulette, Crisis Past or Crisis Future? A Colloquy with Ted C. Fishman, Jeffrey E. Garten, and William Grieder," *Harper's,* June 1998, page 40.

27. Richard Halloran, "China: Restoring the Middle Kingdom," *Parameters: US Army War College Quarterly*, Summer 1998, page 64. Background comments during workshop sponsored by the Asia-Pacific Center for Security Studies, Honolulu, 12-14 January 1998.

28. Bill Powell, quoting Roger Altman in *The New York Times,* "The Other Asian Time Bomb, *Newsweek,* 1 June 1998, pages 42-43.

29. Fareed Zakaria, "How to Be a Great Power Cheap," *Newsweek*, 25 May 1998, page 34.

30. Bruce B. Auster, "An Explosion of Indian Pride," *U.S. News & World Report*, 25 May 1998, pages 16-17.

31. Yehezekel Dror, "High-Intensity Aggressive Ideologies as an International Threat," *Jerusalem Quarterly of International Relations* 9, no. 1 (March 1987): 153-172, cited in Nolan and Strauss, pages 26-27.

32. Robert D. Kaplan, *The Ends of the Earth: From Togo to Turkmenistan, From Iran to Cambodia—A Journey to the Frontiers of Anarchy* (New York, NY: Vintage Books, 1996), page 107.

33. "U.S. General: Nuclear Deterrence Offsets Need for Missile Defense," *Aviation Week and Space Technology*, 2 September 1996, page 8, cited in Nolan and Strauss, page 24.

34. Benjamin R. Barber, *Jihad vs. McWorld: How Globalism and Tribalism Are Reshaping the World* (New York, NY: Ballantine Books, 1996), page 10.

35. Jeffrey B. White, "Irregular Warfare: A Different Kind of Threat," *American Intelligence Journal*, 1996, Volume 17, Nos. 1 & 2, pages 59 and 62.

36. Kaplan, *The Ends of the Earth*, page 23.

CHAPTER 10—THE END OF LIFE AS WE KNOW IT: THE BEGINNING OF LIFE AS WE KNOW IT SHOULD BE

1. I am borrowing the phrase "special moment in history" from Bill McKibben, "A Special Moment in History," *The Atlantic Monthly*, May 1998 article. My usage is somewhat different, obviously, from his.
2. Lesslie Newbigin, *The Gospel in a Pluralist Society* (Grand Rapids, MI: Eerdmans, 1989), page 101.
3. Gordon Humphrey, "Moral Values Central Issue in Presidential Race," *NFD Journal*, November/December 1987, page 10.
4. Allan Bloom, quoting Saul Bellow, *The Closing of the American Mind: How Higher Education Has Failed Democracy and Impoverished the Souls of Today's Students* (New York, NY: Simon and Schuster, 1987), pages 84 and 85.
5. Jim Taylor and Watts Wacker, with Howard Means, *The 500-Year Delta: What Happens After What Comes Next* (New York, NY: HarperBusiness, 1996), pages 67, 68, and 163.
6. Charles Colson, *Loving God* (Grand Rapids, MI: Zondervan, 1983), page 176.
7. George Sanchez, "Watch Out for the Big Squeeze," *Discipleship Journal*, Issue 18, 1983, pages 32-33.
8. Cardinal Suhard, Archbishop of Paris, "Not for Charity," *Kosmos*, September/October 1987, page 27.
9. Nicolas Berdyaev, *The Fate of Man in the Modern World* (Ann Arbor, MI: The University of Michigan Press, 1969, written in 1935), page 130.

AUTHOR

RICHARD A. SWENSON, M.D., received his B.S. in physics Phi Beta Kappa from Denison University (1970) and his doctorate from the University of Illinois School of Medicine (1974). Following five years of private practice, in 1982 Dr. Swenson accepted a teaching position as Associate Clinical Professor with the University of Wisconsin Medical School where he taught for fifteen years. His current focus is "cultural medicine," researching the intersection of faith, health, culture, and the future.

Dr. Swenson has traveled extensively, including a year of study in Europe and medical work in developing countries. He also authored *Margin: Restoring Emotional, Physical, Financial, and Time Reserves to Overloaded Lives* (NavPress, 1992) and *The Overload Syndrome: Learning to Live Within Your Limits* (NavPress, 1998). He has presented widely in both national and international settings on the theme of margin, stress, overload, complexity, and societal change. A representative listing of presentations includes a wide variety of career, professional, and management groups, most major church denominations, Congress, and the Pentagon. In addition, he was an invited guest participant for the 44th Annual National Security Seminar.

PRESCRIPTIONS FOR STRESS FROM DR. RICHARD SWENSON.

Margin

Are you worn out? This book offers healthy living in four areas we all struggle with—emotional energy, physical energy, time, and finances—and will prepare you to live a balanced life.

Margin
$12

The Overload Syndrome

Feeling overwhelmed? Examine the nature of this common problem and learn practical tools for managing overload in the most foundational areas of your life.

The Overload Syndrome
$12

Restoring Margin to Overloaded Lives

Feeling pressured by life? Work through the issues that overload you using this interactive guide. Based on Dr. Richard Swenson's bestselling book *Margin* and its companion book, *The Overload Syndrome*. For groups or individuals.

Restoring Margin to Overloaded Lives
$12

Get your copies today at your local bookstore, through our website, or by calling (800) 366-7788. Ask for offer **#6022** or a FREE catalog of NavPress resources.

NAVPRESS
BRINGING TRUTH TO LIFE
www.navpress.com

Prices subject to change.